D1565794

North Korea

The further a society drifts from the truth the more it will hate those who speak it.

George Orwell

North Korea

Warring with the World

Paul Moorcraft

Pen & Sword
MILITARY

First published in Great Britain in 2020 by
Pen & Sword Military
An imprint of
Pen & Sword Books Ltd
Yorkshire – Philadelphia

Copyright © Paul Moorcraft 2020

ISBN 978 1 52675 946 7

A CIP catalogue record for this book is
available from the British Library.

Typeset by Mac Style
Printed and bound in the UK by TJ International Ltd,
Padstow, Cornwall.

Pen & Sword Books Limited incorporates the imprints of Atlas,
Archaeology, Aviation, Discovery, Family History, Fiction, History,
Maritime, Military, Military Classics, Politics, Select, Transport,
True Crime, Air World, Frontline Publishing, Leo Cooper, Remember
When, Seaforth Publishing, The Praetorian Press, Wharncliffe
Local History, Wharncliffe Transport, Wharncliffe True Crime
and White Owl.

For a complete list of Pen & Sword titles please contact

PEN & SWORD BOOKS LIMITED
47 Church Street, Barnsley, South Yorkshire, S70 2AS, England
E-mail: enquiries@pen-and-sword.co.uk
Website: www.pen-and-sword.co.uk

Or

PEN AND SWORD BOOKS
1950 Lawrence Rd, Havertown, PA 19083, USA
E-mail: Uspen-and-sword@casematepublishers.com
Website: www.penandswordbooks.com

Contents

For Sarah

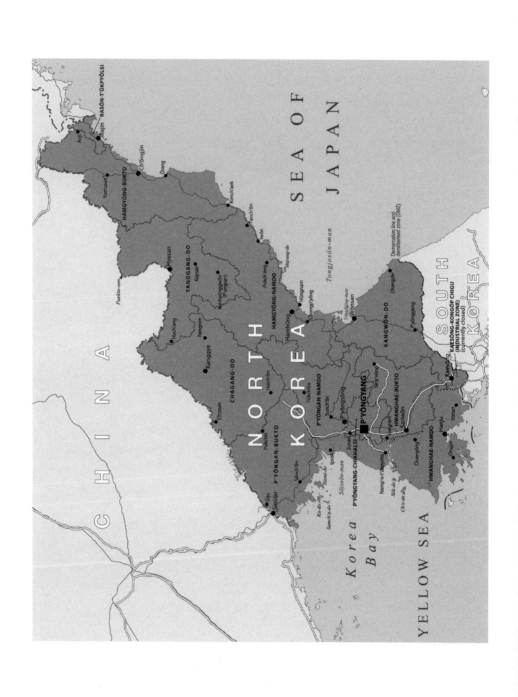

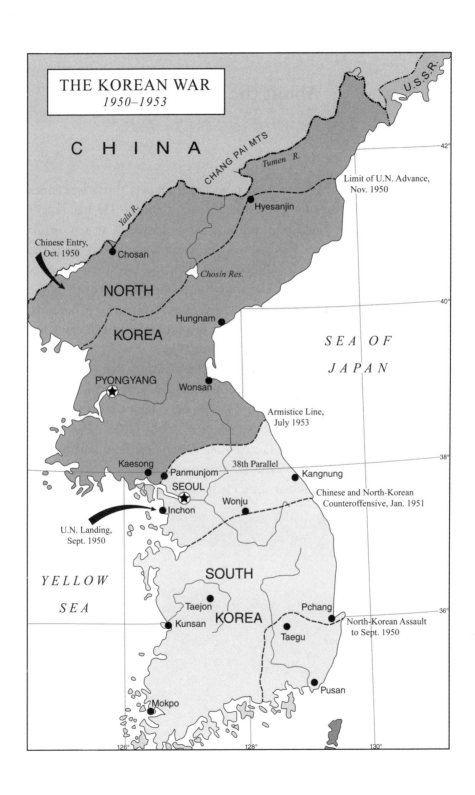

THE KOREAN WAR
1950–1953

CHINA

U.S.S.R.

CHANG PAI MTS

Tumen R.

Yalu R.

Limit of U.N. Advance,
Nov. 1950

Chinese Entry,
Oct. 1950

Hyesanjin

Chosan

Chosin Res.

NORTH

Hungnam

KOREA

SEA OF

JAPAN

PYONGYANG

Wonsan

Armistice Line,
July 1953

Kaesong
Panmunjom
38th Parallel
Kangnung

SEOUL

Chinese and North-Korean
Counteroffensive, Jan. 1951

Wonju

U.N. Landing,
Sept. 1950

Inchon

YELLOW

SOUTH

SEA

Taejon
KOREA
Pchang

North-Korean Assault
to Sept. 1950

Kunsan

Taegu

Pusan

Mokpo

42°

40°

38°

36°

126°
128°
130°

About the Author

Professor Paul Moorcraft has reported from over thirty war zones over forty years for print and broadcast media. He has taught politics and journalism fulltime (consecutively) at ten major international universities. For five years he was a senior instructor at the Royal Military Academy, Sandhurst, and then the UK Joint Services Command and Staff College. The author also worked extensively in the Ministry of Defence in Whitehall and in various theatres. Dr Moorcraft, who ran a think tank dedicated to conflict resolution for fifteen years, has travelled and worked extensively throughout Asia.

The author of numerous works on military history, his most recent books for Pen and Sword include *The Rhodesian War* (2015), *Superpowers, Rogue States and Terrorism* (2016), *The Jihadist Threat* (2017) and *Total Onslaught: War and Revolution in Southern Africa* (2018). His fourth volume of memoirs was *Deadlines on the Front Line* (Pen and Sword, 2018). He is the author of award-winning novels and non-fiction books on crime as well as on mathematics. He lives in a riverside cottage in the UK's Surrey Hills.

Timeline

1875	Japan invades Korea
1894–5	Japan defeats Chinese attempts to intervene
1904–5	Japan defeats Russia
1910	Japan annexes Korea
1919	First major Korean nationalist resistance
1925	Formation of the Korean Communist Party in Seoul
1929	Anti-Japanese demonstrations spread throughout the peninsula
1931	Japanese invade Manchuria
1938	December, Japan declares the Greater East Asia Co-Prosperity Sphere, outline of new empire
1940	September, Japanese move into China. Vichy France capitulates to Japanese and allows them to station imperial troops in French Indo-China
1941	December, Japan attacks US forces at Pearl Harbor
1945	February, At Yalta US, UK and USSR agree to a post-war trusteeship of Korea
	August, Atomic bombs dropped on Japan
1945–48	Soviet administration
1948	Beginning of Kim Il-sung regime
1950–53	Korean War
1966–69	DMZ conflict ('Second Korean War')
1994	Death of Kim Il-sung; Kim Jong-il takes over
1994–98	Worst years of famine
1998	Beginning of 'sunshine policy'
2002	USA brands North Korea as part of the 'axis of evil'
2003	Six-party talks
2006	(9 October) First DPRK nuclear test
2009	Second test
2010	ROKS *Cheonan* sinking

2011	Death of Kim Jong-il; Kim Jong-un takes over
2013	Third nuclear test
2017	Serious threat of nuclear war
2018	Kim Jong-un becomes first North Korean leader to enter the south when he meets South Korean President Moon Jae-in for talks. Weeks later he meets US President Donald Trump in Singapore.
2019	Donald Trump meets Kim Jong-un in Hanoi (February); and the two leaders meet again in the DMZ (June).

The Leaders

Kim Il-sung (1948–94)
Kim Jong-il (1994–2011)
Kim Jong-un (2011–present)

Glossary of Abbreviations

BCFK   British Commonwealth Forces, Korea
COIN   Counter-insurgency
DMZ   The Demilitarized Zone, an armistice line that divides the peninsula
DPRK   Democratic People's Republic of Korea – North Korea
HDRF   Homeland Defense Reserve Force
IAEA   International Atomic Energy Authority
KOMID   Korean Mining and Development Corporation
KPA   Korean People's Army (North Korea)
KPISF   Korean People's Internal Security Forces
NLL   Northern Limit Line
NNSC   Neutral Nations Supervisory Commission
PAF   People's Armed Forces (North Korea)
PDS   Public Distribution System
PLA   People's Liberation Army (China)
PRC   People's Republic of China (Communist China)
ROK   Republic of Korea; South Korea
ROKA   Republic of Korea's Army
THAAD   Terminal High Altitude Area Defence
USSR   Union of Soviet Socialist Republics

Glossary of Terms

Arduous March:	The official name for the food emergency in the 1990s (originally the period when Japanese imperial forces were hunting Kim Il-sung)
Chongryon:	Japanese of Korean descent
Chosun:	North Korea's name for the country
Dear Leader:	Kim Jong-il
Great Leader:	Kim Il-sung or Kim Jong-il
Janmadang:	informal market
Juche:	North Korean policy of self-reliance
Michenom:	'American imperialist bastard'
People's Volunteer Army:	The name given to Chinese regular forces fighting in Korea.
Songbun:	Caste system in North Korea
Songun:	Military-first policy
Southern *Chosun*:	North Korean name for the south
Sunshine policy:	Southern rapprochement with North Korea
Supreme Leader:	Kim Il-sung
Won:	unit of currency

Introduction: The Mouse that Roared

I first became aware of the conflicts on the Korean peninsula when my father, as a reservist, was put on standby to serve there with the Royal Air Force in 1950. And the chimera – or reality – of a quintessential threat posed by North Korea to the West seemed to hover in the background throughout my life. In my many travels in Asia, especially working in China and Indo-China, the ghost of possible nuclear vengeance haunted my political imagination. Sometimes the threat was made substantive, when, for example, I was working on North Korea's active military support for the Tamil Tigers in Sri Lanka. When I wrote an inside account of that conflict, the most devious and active external backer in supplying arms and equipment to one of the most ingenious (and deadly) of the world's rebel movements was Pyongyang. As a journalist, academic and later, during my service for the UK Ministry of Defence, the potential dangers of North Korea's nuclear programme always lurked somewhere in the background, and more recently in the foreground.

The dynastic rulers of the so-called hermit kingdom have always been portrayed as evil and ruthless and usually insane as well. They were sometimes considered mad and bad enough to actually use their nukes once they had developed them. In fact this book explains the sane logic of the North Korean position. The rulers of a tiny country with many enemies and just a few allies, albeit one being the new superpower, China, played a poor hand well, and with consistency, over decades. The regime survives, despite all the odds. And, with the advent of US President Donald Trump, the current ruler of the Democratic People's Republic of Korea, Kim Jong-un, arguably appears, by comparison, especially sane.

I shall attempt to dissect the logic of the North Korean position and consider the prospects for peace on the Korean peninsula. The major powers fought the first limited war in the nuclear age from 1950–53.

Technically that war has not ended: an armistice, *not* a peace treaty, was agreed in 1953. The two countries are technically still at war (though north and south have recently rowed back from that legal position). In 2017–early 2018 it looked as though war could break out by accident or intent as President Trump ratcheted up the military stakes. Then the leaders of north and south started a renewed 'sunshine' dialogue; and in 2018 Mr Trump met Mr Kim face to face and they seemed to get on tolerably well, though the second direct bilateral summit in 2019 fared less well.

The question of the Korean peninsula's status and then the bellicosity of North Korea have been a thorn in the flesh of the West since the end of the Second World War. The hostility erupted into a major war in the 1950s and teetered on the edge of another major international confrontation once North Korea had showcased its nuclear credentials. At the time of writing, the thaw with the West and with the South suggests some grounds for optimism. Domestically, North Korea's citizens have suffered a regime that has created or allowed famine and mass repression. My account is no apologia for a remarkably cruel government. What I am trying to do is explain how the tiny 'communist' state has survived and to ask whether real peace and even reunification could be generated on the Korean peninsula.

'North Korea was created by revolutionaries driven by nationalism, anti-imperialism and the search for the right path to modernity.'[1] So it is important to understand North Korea's origins. The ruling party derives from the small group of partisans who were trained by the NKVD/KGB and the Comintern and, later, the Chinese communists to fight the Japanese army that occupied Korea from 1910 to 1945. The Democratic People's Republic of Korea (DPRK) was born in Japanese brutality and it still responds brutally to threats. Its rogue status is not just because of nuclear weapons. It produces and smuggles forged currency and narcotics on an industrial scale. Besides its leading role in cyber-terrorism, North Korea has a vast small-arms industry. As I said, I spent more than a year investigating, inter alia, the DPRK's involvement with arming the Tamil Tigers for my book on the war in Sri Lanka. The DPRK has energetic spy rings around the world, sometimes kidnapping people to work in the hermit kingdom, most infamously to help its film industry and espionage schools. It has conducted well-known assassinations abroad, most recently Kim Jong-un's half-brother in Kuala Lumpur's international airport. It stifles even the mildest internal dissent ruthlessly. There may be up to 200,000 political prisoners in horrific camps. Ideologically it is in some respects the last hold-out of Stalinism. Despite all the apparatus of a communist party, it is in reality a neo-Confucian feudal kingdom run by a dynasty now in its third generation. Even Stalin did not try to elevate one of his sons as an heir. And yet the dynasty is not completely secure – the power behind the throne is the military. The hardline generals naturally support the state philosophy of military first. They are committed to the unification of the peninsula, by any means. Nukes help here. Also, as the regime looks at the downfall of Libya's Colonel Gaddafi it concludes that the Colonel, and Saddam Hussein before him, might have survived if they could have wielded the threat of atomic bombs.

In short, the regime leaders may be bad but they are not mad. There is method in their over-the-top rhetoric about frying their enemies. The Chinese are their sole real, if sometimes lukewarm, friends and only play at sanctions as PR for Beijing's international image. The Chinese pretend to stop coal imports moving north or oil going south (temporarily). Washington, in contrast, stopped any hints of Taiwan or South Korea securing a nuclear weapon but as late as 2012 North Korea was publicly displaying huge Chinese-built missile launchers in Pyongyang's military parades. Even if Beijing decided to cut the life support it may be that the North Korean military would not listen to China and replace President Kim if he looked like making a real deal with Trump ... or even Beijing. That is the danger of dealing with such an apparently volatile and certainly secretive regime – it is very unpredictable to outsiders (despite its internal logic to the small ruling elite).

Washington has often urged China to take the lead, and also Moscow, which has some, but far less, influence. That is the problem with letting a rogue country develop nuclear weapons. It is probably too late to use pre-emptive military power against Pyongyang. In that sense, North Korea has won. They have behaved dangerously but not insanely.

British filmmaker John Sweeney wrote a book about his unauthorized journalism in North Korea. He said:

Understanding North Korea is like figuring out a detective story, where you stumble across a corpse in the library, a smoking gun beside it, and the corpse gets up and says that's no gun, and it isn't smoking and this isn't a library. It is like nowhere else on earth.[2]

The point of this book is to reveal the truth behind the detective story. And, along the way, there are lots of smoking guns to wave.

Chapter 1

The Origins of the North Korean State

Before the nineteenth century Korea was often consumed with civil wars between various indigenous kingdoms, though some progress was achieved – not least metal-block printing long before its advent in Europe. Inevitably economic and scientific advances were often imperilled by external invasions, first from the Mongols, then later from Chinese and Japanese interventions.

The Americans also made various forceful attempts to trade with the isolationist Korea in the second half of the nineteenth century. In August 1866 an American ship, the heavily-armed *General Sherman*, along with some Chinese junks, entered the Taedong river. After a series of incidents the American ship was burned and the crew members were killed. An investigative/retaliatory US naval expedition in 1871 followed when hundreds of Koreans were killed for the loss of three Americans. This was the first major American military action in Korea.

Imperial Japan wiped out much of the Chinese influence in Korea after the first Sino-Japanese conflict (1894–95). Ten years later, in the war between the empires of Japan and Russia, the Russians were heavily defeated, first with the fall of their mighty stronghold at Port Arthur and then with a major defeat on land in Manchuria (the Battle of Mukden) and in the Strait of Tsushima where Tsar Nicholas II's fleet was almost completely annihilated. This was the first time that an Asian state had defeated a modern Western country; it disabused – or *should* have disabused – the great European powers of their racist assumptions. Port Arthur was considered to be one of the best fortified places in the world. Its fall prefigured the fighting in the twentieth century, especially the First World War. The siege of Port Arthur included massive howitzers, machine guns, barbed wire, electric fences and searchlights, plus extensive trench warfare. More significantly the Russian defeats were an early portent of the end of the European empires. Ironically, it also boosted Japanese notions of racial supremacy that were to survive until the American domination of the island nation in 1945.

Under the Treaty of Eulsa in 1905 Korea was made a protectorate of Japan and the country was annexed in 1910. The Japanese were to rule the Korean peninsula with a heavy hand from 1910 to the end of the Second World War. The atomic bomb attacks on Hiroshima and Nagasaki in August 1945 dramatically ended the occupation. The Japanese had developed some industry but the majority of Koreans were subsistence farmers. A Korean resistance movement had developed slowly in the mountainous areas and in neighbouring Manchuria. One of the most well-known guerrilla leaders was Kim Il-sung, a communist stalwart. Under Japanese imperial rule, the country was little influenced by the main currents of Western thought, though the arrival of Christian missionaries in the eighteenth and nineteenth centuries had had a big impact, especially in the north.

Many Korean nationalists fled the iron-fisted Japanese rule. In 1919 the nationalists set up a provisional government in China but internal squabbling made it ineffective. The Korean communists were more unified and they formed the backbone to the Korean insurgency against imperial Japan. Both the nationalist Kuomintang and the Chinese Red Army helped to organize the pockets of Korean resistance against the Japanese army. During the Second World War, at the Cairo conference in November 1943, the Western Allies declared that, after the war, Korea would become independent. Some of the Kuomintang-backed Korean forces fought in Burma against the Japanese while the communist-backed Koreans fought both in Korea and in Manchuria.

Joseph Stalin had promised his Western allies that he would enter the war against Japan not later than three months after the victory over Nazism in Europe. Moscow kept its word and declared war on Japan on 8 August 1945. The USSR had all the advantages, not least its territorial contiguity to Korea, although the Red Army rapidly controlled the north after amphibious landings. Washington feared that the Soviets would take the whole peninsula and so the Americans suggested a Soviet occupation zone above the 38th Parallel. The US Army would control the south, although US forces did not arrive in strength until 8 September. To Washington's surprise the Russians accepted the deal. Stalin maintained his wartime policy of co-operation with his Western allies and ordered his Red Army troops to halt at the 38th Parallel to await the late arrival of US forces. This meant that Washington was in charge of the capital, Seoul, and 16 million Koreans, while the Red Army controlled 9 million of the Korean population in the north.

Koreans were hardly consulted at all about the division of their country by the Soviets and Americans. When the Japanese emperor announced his country's surrender on the radio on 15 August 1945 the vast majority of Koreans were taken by surprise. The Japanese imperial authorities had closely controlled media access to the war, not least accounts of recent Japanese reverses. Koreans were stunned by the news but soon mass celebrations took place; then followed an orgy of destruction against all symbols of Japanese rule, especially the Shinto shrines to which they had been forced to pay their respects. Koreans – north and south – began to plan for their independence as a new state. Their joy was short-lived as the Americans had other plans – hastily contrived, it was true, but very distinct from Korean aspirations.

The Americans assumed that the Soviets had a detailed blueprint for their zone of occupation. And yet the post-Cold War opening of the Soviet archives has shown how ill-prepared the Soviets were too. Moscow saw the problem as a military one and so left it to the generals, especially Colonel General Terentii Shtykov, who ran the occupation and later became the first Soviet ambassador to the DPRK. Both the Russians and the Americans had come to fight the Japanese, not govern Koreans. Despite isolated acts of rape and pillage, the Russians soon established order and did rather better at working with the local Koreans, especially the small number of communists and well-educated Christians, than the Americans in the south who initially over-relied on the existing Japanese or Japanese-trained authorities.

US Lieutenant General John Reed Hodge was the military governor of South Korea from 1945 until 1948 under the United States Army Military Government in Korea (USAMGIK). He had received the surrender of all Japanese forces in Korea south of the 38th Parallel. Hodge tried initially to rule through Japanese colonial institutions but met with fierce Korean protests. It was much easier for Americans to relate to disciplined fellow soldiers – even Japanese enemies – than try to deal with the apparently anarchistic Koreans swamped in endless and complicated political fratricides. The Americans generally knew little or nothing about Korean culture and initially had to rely on Japanese expertise and translators. Even when Japanese officials were shipped home, the Americans tended to rely on Koreans, especially in the police, who had been trained by Japanese imperial officers.

Lieutenant General Hodge did not recognize the short-lived People's Republic of Korea set up in the south because of its suspected communist leanings. The divided country was supposed to be administered by a US/USSR Joint Commission with the aim of granting independence after a five-year trusteeship. Many Koreans, north and south, did not want to wait – they'd had enough of alien rule, both harsh and recently relatively benign, but rule by foreigners nonetheless. After extensive protests and strikes, the American overlords declared martial law. Facing an impasse, Washington decided to hold a general election under UN auspices. The Soviets and many Koreans, including some in the south, boycotted the May 1948 election. Syngman Rhee was elected president in July 1948 and the Republic of Korea (South Korea) was set up in the following August. In the north the Soviets established a communist government led by their man, Kim Il-sung. The Russian occupation forces left the north by the end of 1948, while the USA withdrew its troops in 1949.

If Kim Il-sung was Moscow's protégé, Syngman Rhee was equally Washington's man. He had a long track record of nationalism, not least in opposition to the Japanese. He had been jailed and later spent many years in exile in the USA. Syngman Rhee was a Christian anti-communist and spoke excellent English, a big bonus for the largely monoglot US soldiers, intelligence officers and diplomats who dealt with him. As a British diplomat noted at the time, 'The Americans frequently go for a man, rather than a movement.' The classic example was the US support for Chiang Kai-shek in the civil war in China. This pattern was to be repeated throughout the Cold War, notably in the 'third world', where Americans, especially the Central Intelligence Agency, tended to back their man on the principle that 'he may be a sonofabitch but he's *our* sonofabitch'.

The US State Department had misgivings about Syngman Rhee but American military intelligence, especially the military governors, had backed him. This was the time of the emerging Truman Doctrine, when President Harry S. Truman had pledged to 'contain' the advance of communism, not least in Asia and in China in particular. The 'domino theory' was also coming into fashion: 'lose' one pro-Western state and the rest in the neighbourhood would soon topple over. Syngman Rhee, despite his feisty and authoritarian temperament, was considered the least worst choice for the Americans.

In the north the Soviet Red Army had worked with the various people's committees, including those set up by leading Christian nationalists. Local nationalists had already declared a People's Republic of Korea. The Russians promoted Kim Il-sung as a national hero because he and a small group of Korean officers had fought in the Red Army. Some had lived in the USSR since the 1930s and been trained by the Soviets; they fought the Japanese in Manchuria and later the Kuomintang Chinese forces. Over 50,000 Koreans had fought alongside the Chinese communist People's Liberation Army. Although Moscow promoted Kim Il-sung, the Russians also considered other Korean leaders. The Workers' Party of North Korea was founded in 1946 and later incorporated various popular fronts, north and south, to form the Workers' Party of Korea with Kim Il-sung as chairman.

Most of the local communists who had survived Japanese occupation were peasants and not Marxist-trained leaders from the proletariat. The few local supporters of the Russian model of revolution were pushed aside. As a result, the leadership of North Korea came almost entirely from people who had largely lived their adult lives outside the north: in Manchuria, South Korea or the USSR. In many cases they had not lived in what became the DPRK until after the 'liberation'. The Soviets liked people they knew and trusted and Kim Il-sung could also speak Russian.

Moscow was applying the tried and tested Bolshevik methodology that Stalin applied in all his satellites: to create almost identical political and military structures in the Marxist-Leninist mode. Moscow also tended to promote similar personality types as leaders: administratively able, ruthless, authoritarian and usually paranoid. The ossified groupthink of the North Korean leadership today is a testament to the durable efficacy of Stalin's methodology. In Korea, at the end of the Second World War, the consolidation of communist power by forging popular fronts repeated what happened in most of the Soviet bloc. In Eastern Europe, especially in Poland and Czechoslovakia in 1948–49, smaller communist parties merged with larger and more popular socialist parties. The Korean communist party was like its Chinese counterpart. Ideologically, that posed a challenge to the Kremlin in the 1950s and 1960s. Mao had torn up the Bolshevik rule book by mobilizing the peasantry and ignoring China's small urban proletariat, the opposite of how the communists had built their base in Russia.

Kim Il-sung was prompted by the Russians to form the Korean People's Army (KPA). The hard core of the new force consisted of veterans who had gained combat experience fighting both the Japanese and Kuomintang. Moscow provided advisers and equipment from the vast Soviet arsenal that had been constructed to defeat Adolf Hitler. The KPA expanded, with Chinese as well as Russian largesse, and was soon bristling with relatively modern Soviet military equipment, including tanks and aircraft. In the Soviet-controlled north the Stalinist model was replicated in the economy thus creating a state-controlled infrastructure.

Land reform came first in the north: land belonging to the ejected Japanese and Korean 'traitors' (collaborators with the imperial occupiers) was re-allocated to a grateful peasantry while in the south traditional landlords mostly held sway. In the north women were given equal rights in what had been a deeply patriarchal society. All in the north were urged not to use conventional forms of address and instead deploy the term 'comrade'. Education was prioritized and Moscow's money helped to build up the industrial base.

The different zones of occupation soon hardened into separate political systems. As the Cold War froze Europe into two camps, so, too, in Korea co-operation between the USA and USSR broke down, especially over the question of elections throughout the peninsula. Separate elections were held in the south in May 1948; in the following August the Republic of Korea was declared in the south, while, in the north, the Democratic People's Republic of Korea (DPRK) was established in September. It was a fully-fledged communist state with Kim Il-sung as dictator. He would rule the new state with an iron fist until his death in 1994. The powerful North Korean military was determined to restore unity of the homeland, by force if necessary.

Kim Il-sung believed that a North Korean army would be welcomed in the south as liberators. Regular border clashes ensued, often with the northern forces coming out on top. Kim asked Stalin for his permission to invade the south. The Soviet dictator, however, was initially reluctant. But the fact that the US did not go all out to back nationalist forces in China suggested to Stalin that the Americans would be even less likely to go to war over Korea, which had far less strategic importance. Washington was indeed unsure about its commitment to the troublesome entity in the south of the peninsula. The most famous example of this ambiguity was Secretary of State Dean Acheson's speech at Washington's National Press Club on 12 January 1950 in which he excluded South Korea from the USA's defence perimeter. The Soviets were also reading the coded communications between Washington and the US embassy in Moscow. The Americans were not likely to risk nuclear confrontation – Moscow had tested its first atomic weapon on 29 August 1949 – over tiny and poor Korea. Moscow also signed a whole series of economic and military pacts with the new and triumphant communist government in Beijing.

The tectonic plates had shifted in Asia when Mao's communists finally defeated the American-backed nationalist forces and declared the People's Republic of China on 1 October 1949. The remnants of the rival Kuomintang forces fled to Taiwan to set up the Republic of China. US military support has enabled Taiwan to survive as an independent state to this day, despite the overwhelming power of the next-door People's Republic. Unifying China – first incorporating Tibet – became the leitmotif of Beijing, just as unification had once dominated the DPRK.

Weighing up the strategic balance of power, in early 1950, Stalin gave Kim Il-sung the go-ahead, provided the Chinese promised to provide reinforcements if they were required. Mao Zedong needed the support of the Russian alliance in the early days of his rule. More ethnic Koreans in China were drafted into Kim's forces and then regular detachments of the PLA were moved closer to the border. Senior Red Army generals in the Soviet Advisory Group advised the North Koreans how to over-run the fledgling imperialist-ruled southern state.

Kim called for a nationwide election and offered various peace overtures that the south rejected. Meanwhile, clashes along the 38th Parallel, some initiated by the southern forces, increased in tempo. The over-confidence of the American military trainers had infused the South Korean generals. The commander of the US Military Advisory Group, General William L. Roberts, asserted that a northern invasion would merely provide 'target practice'. Although some US intelligence officers feared a 'little China' in Korea, most focused on the more immediate threat to Formosa/Taiwan. The defeated nationalist forces, the Kuomintang, had been forced to relocate there under the umbrella of American military power. One of the most infamous of the Cambridge spies, Guy Burgess, may well have worked hard to conjure up the danger to Taiwan as a diversion from the real thrust into South Korea. Burgess was appointed to the Far East Department of MI6 in 1948.

Syngman Rhee also boasted of his desire to conquer the north. In addition, the CIA suggested in May 1950 that northern manoeuvres were 'defensive' and on 23 June UN observers visiting the borders said war was not imminent.

The CIA and UN experts were wrong. The North Korean forces stood at perhaps nearly 200,000. They were well-organized and well-armed. They had just under 300 Soviet tanks as well as perhaps 150 fighters, mainly Yak-3 and Lavochkin La-7 piston-engined fighters as well as Ilyushin Il-10 ground-attack aircraft, the highly regarded Shturmoviks. The southern army had fewer than 100,000 troops and no tanks, and they had only a tiny air force. Yes, the Americans had large garrisons in Japan and major fleets and a powerful air force but only around 250 US combat troops were actually on the ground in South Korea. American hubris was about to be swamped by its nemesis in the shape of the North Korean blitzkrieg.

Chapter 2

The Korean War

The course of the war

On 24 June 1950 the West discovered that the Cold War was suddenly turning very hot when communist North Korea invaded South Korea. For three years, under the banner of the United Nations, the West fought the most bloodily direct campaign of the Cold War. As the years of East-West conflict rolled on, it was so rare to find American troops fighting Russian or Chinese soldiers face to face. Despite the UN appellation, this was essentially an American-led war to defend the south. It was initially headed by some commanders who threatened atomic weapons but who in the end did not use them. Although Washington feared that the fall of the pro-Western, corrupt South Korea would constitute a domino that would tip other Asian states into the communist camp, it was not a war of survival to parallel the Second World War. And yet it could still have led to the first – and presumably last – nuclear war between the Russians and Americans.

The communist leaderships in both Moscow and Beijing backed North Korean supremo Kim Il-sung while the Western powers, led by Washington, supported the regime of Syngman Rhee in Seoul. Both Kim Il-sung and Syngman Rhee claimed to head the sole legitimate government of *all* Korea. Clashes had become more frequent over the post-1945 temporary border with both sides blaming each other. When the North Korean armed forces finally swept over the demarcation boundaries, the United Nations Security Council authorized the formation of UN forces to repel the invasion from the north. The UN forces eventually comprised twenty-one countries, though 90 per cent were American military personnel.

The North Korean invasion had taken the Americans by surprise. The new superpower had downsized from 12 million men and women in uniform in 1945 to about 1.6 million in 1950. True, the US Army had over 100,000 troops occupying Japan but they were largely clerks and administrators, not combat troops. But these were the first to be sent to South Korea. Initially the UN forces were pushed into a small area in the south known as the Pusan Perimeter. The atomically-armed American superpower faced conventional defeat. In September 1950, however, a bold amphibious UN counter-offensive was launched at Inchon. British historian Max Hastings noted that the US Marine Corps had many officers with lots of knowledge about opposed amphibious landings. 'These men understood from experience every subtlety of tides, beach gradients, unloading capacity, and fire support plans.'

The North Korean invaders found themselves cut off and surrounded by MacArthur's forces and retreated in haste and confusion towards the Yalu river, the border with the newly established People's Republic of China. After the DPRK catastrophe at Inchon, it looked as though Stalin was going to give up on his new Asian protégé. That is one of the reasons why Kim Il-sung began to shift towards Beijing. Only the year before, Mao Zedong's communist party had triumphed in the long civil war. The victorious Chinese People's Liberation Army, which included many Kuomintang conscripts, had not been demobilized. In October 1950 the mass surprise intervention of experienced Chinese forces pushed back the UN armies. In the dramatic and rapid changes of fortune during the three-year war, Seoul changed hands four times. A war of attrition ensued with the front line usually standing near the 38th Parallel.

The air war was much more dynamic. To inflict the greatest possible destruction on the communist forces, the UN launched a massive bombing campaign in Korea. The war also saw the first aerial combat between jet aircraft. US Air Force pilots flying in Lockheed F-80 Shooting Stars and F-86 Sabres fought dog-fights with North Korean MiG-15s flown by Soviet pilots.

The war was fought savagely for three years until July 1953. An armistice was signed though it was not until 2018 that serious negotiations attempted to end the legal fact that technically both sides were still at war. The south has traditionally called the war the '625 upheaval' relating to the onset of war on 25 June. The north typically refers to the 'Fatherland Liberation War'. Beijing called the conflict the 'War to Resist America and Aid Korea'. Washington used the term 'police action' initially and never formally declared war, as the USA fought under the banner of the UN. Western historians have tended to dub the 1950–53 Korean conflict as the 'forgotten war', because it was fought largely in an era when news travelled very slowly compared to the war in Vietnam more than a decade in the future. Print journalism and the cinema newsreels were in their heyday but Western reporters and cameramen were subject (later) to strict censorship. With no live TV reporting in existence at the time the war in Korea could appear to be a long way away to members of the public in the West – unless of course they had husbands, brothers and sons fighting there.

Key military aspects of the war

The North Korean forces launched a well-organized all-arms attack on Sunday 25 June 1950. The clear-cut aggression of a naked invasion helped fuel some popular enthusiasm in the democratic West for such an uncertain cause over three years. In the short term, the South Koreans – ill-armed – fought a piecemeal defensive action. It was so hapless that the capital fell in three days. Most of the government fled south, led by Syngman Rhee, whom the North dubbed the 'bandit traitor'. What was left of the South Korean forces came under UN, effectively American, command, in early July. Initially Washington had thought that its air and naval assets would be enough.

On 27 June the UN Security Council, which had been temporarily boycotted by the USSR, passed Resolution 83 allowing for military assistance to South Korea. Meanwhile the Republic of Korea (ROK) army was in full flight south or simply defecting to the northern side. At the same time – assuming that it might be part of a general communist advance in Europe and Asia – the US sent in its Seventh Fleet to defend the island of Taiwan, where the remnants of the Kuomintang had set up an anti-communist regime.

Initial US troop deployments were overwhelmed. At the battle of Taejon, the American 24th Division suffered just over 3,500 killed and wounded and nearly 3,000 captured including the US commander, Major General William F. Dean. He was an unlucky officer, who had been wounded in a flame-thrower accident in the Second World War and then became the highest-ranking American officer to become a PoW in the Korean War. He had been badly wounded and was then continually ill because of poor food but he refused to succumb to his interrogators despite being kept in solitary confinement. Dean was not, however, physically tortured.

Elsewhere the northern forces killed off Korean intellectuals and senior civil servants as they continued their advance. Eventually the UN forces were pushed back to a small corner of south-east Korea, the so-called Pusan Perimeter. Heavy US air bombing started to destroy the logistics of the Korean People's Army (KPA) and the US pushed over 500 medium tanks and fresh troops into the Pusan area.

General Douglas MacArthur turned the tables on the over-extended northern forces. In mid-September, nearly 40,000 Americans from the US Marines and the 7th Infantry Division, plus over 8,000 ROK troops, landed successfully at the lightly defended city of Incheon. Then UN troops broke out of the besieged Pusan Perimeter. The sudden reversal of fortunes caused the Russian and Chinese advisers, who were barely co-ordinating with each other and with the North Koreans, to issue conflicting advice.

On 25 September, Seoul was recaptured. British war correspondent Reginald Thompson described the scene that greeted American troops as they entered the southern capital:

> An appalling inferno of din and destruction with the tearing noise of Corsair dive bombers blasting right ahead, and the livid flashes of the tank guns, the harsh fierce crackle of blazing wooden buildings, telegraph and high-tension poles collapsing in utter chaos of wires … it seemed indeed that 'all hell was let loose' on this city.[1]

Instead of withdrawing to defend the north, many KPA units disintegrated. And now Pyongyang was vulnerable.

On 30 September Beijing warned the USA that if Western troops crossed the 38th Parallel, the Chinese People's Liberation Army would step in. ROK troops began to cross over to chase retreating communist forces. On 7 October UN units moved northwards. The North Korean capital was taken on 19 October. At the end of that month, the UN forces had captured more than 135,000 KPA (Korean People's Army). The UN forces eventually captured around 90 per cent of the DPRK. Such was the UN momentum that Douglas MacArthur wanted to move across the China-North Korean border to knock out supply depots for the North Korean war effort. President Harry Truman, however, ordered MacArthur to stop at the Chinese border. Beijing made it clear – via numerous neutral diplomats – that the Chinese People's Liberation Army would intervene in strength if the UN forces tried to cross into Chinese territory. Stalin made it clear that Soviet forces would not take part directly but encouraged Chairman Mao to send up to six divisions into Korea. For Stalin, the war drained US resources, not least away from Europe, which was his prime concern. And he did not commit any ground troops. He left that to the Chinese who had ample cannon fodder in their bloated armed forces.

Mao had not firmly entrenched his leadership position and he had to use some persuasion in the politburo to ensure intervention in the war. Stalin made it clear that he would not contribute ground combat troops but he did send limited supplies of military equipment and, later, Soviet pilots.

From late October divisions of PLA soldiers marched at night into North Korea, despite General MacArthur's assurance to his president that he did not think the Chinese would move in and, even if they did, they would be 'slaughtered' by superior American air power. US intelligence seemed ignorant of the presence of mass Chinese armies across the border. The disciplined PLA lit no fires for cooking, lay low during the day and so were 'invisible' to the Americans. But secret Chinese infiltration led to direct confrontation with the Americans – and the PLA defeated the US 8th Cavalry Regiment at the Battle of Unsan. This action persuaded Moscow to allow the Soviet air force to provide air cover.

The Chinese did not press their advantage but withdrew into the mountains. With Zhou Enlai as commander, the PLA units – known as the People's Volunteer Army – overran ROK forces at the Battle of the Ch'ongch'on River and then pounded the US 2nd Infantry Division. The US Eighth Army crossed back over the 38th Parallel border in mid-December. They had retreated in the north-west far faster than they had advanced, while in the north-east the evacuation was a little more orderly. Over 100,000 troops and their kit were evacuated to Pusan.

Beijing blamed American aggression, not least air attacks in China, for its rapid and successful intervention in the Korean civil war. On 26 December 1950, in the so-called Chinese New Year offensive, the North Koreans and Chinese launched a series of surprise night attacks, using psychological warfare – blowing trumpets and banging gongs – to disorientate the enemy. As Darrell Bailey, an American NCO who had fought in Western Europe, commented, 'They advanced right into our fire. They were brave.' Both the North Korean and Chinese troops fought with an apparent disregard for their own lives. They deployed Banzai-style surprise attacks, in the mould of the Japanese Imperial Army. Initially the mass suicidal waves caused panic. After the major Chinese counter-attack, panicky withdrawals of American troops became common. It was dubbed 'bug-out fever'. Such was the momentum of the offensive that the communist forces conquered Seoul for the second time on 4 January 1951.

It was at this critical stage in the war that MacArthur pressed Washington to use nuclear weapons to stop the Chinese. Again the communist forces – using primitive logistics of deploying material on bicycles and on foot from the supply depots over the Yalu river border – became overstretched. In late January, the charismatic General Matthew Ridgway took over the demoralized Eighth Army – and later became supreme commander of UN forces in Korea when MacArthur was sacked. Ridgway had served in the Great War and excelled in the Second World War, especially in Normandy and the Battle of the Bulge. Above all, he was credited with turning the war around in Korea. His long and highly successful military career was recognized by the award of the Presidential Medal of Freedom in 1986 by President Ronald Reagan, who said that: 'Heroes come when they're needed; great men step forward when courage seems in short supply.'

In late January 1951 the UN command initiated what became known as Operation THUNDERBOLT which deployed air power to great effect. In the south the police and ROK army conducted various campaigns against guerrillas. Atrocities sometimes ensued, notably the Geochang and Sancheong-Hamyang massacres. In mid-February communist forces launched another offensive but US, ROK and French troops broke the momentum at Chipyong-ni. Nearly 6,000 UN troops were surrounded by over 25,000 opponents. Instead of retreating in the face of massive superiority, they fought and won what is sometimes called 'the Gettysburg of the Korean War'.

At the end of February 1951, Operation THUNDERBOLT was succeeded by Operation KILLER in an attempt to kill as many opposing forces as possible. 'Killing gooks' was the derogative term commonly used then. One British company commander commented that 'the trigger finger became exhausted with killing and his men finished up by pulling the triggers of their weapons with the third, fourth and little fingers'.

After this attritional success, Operation RIPPER expelled North Korean and Chinese forces from Seoul on 14 March. This was the fourth capture of the southern capital, leaving it in ruins.

The northern forces were still suffering from acute logistical problems and Beijing asked Stalin for more air support to protect supply lines. Moscow sent in two air force divisions and three anti-aircraft formations. In addition, around 6,000 trucks were supplied. Also, the Chinese air force began taking part in air combat from September 1951. The conflict had become largely a war of attrition between the US and China with their respective allies playing minor roles.

President Truman wanted a limited war and considered a truce leading to the status quo an acceptable solution, while General MacArthur had wanted a total war and total victory. Congressional hearings in May and June 1951 determined that MacArthur had disobeyed orders, and caused mass casualties, by pushing into Chinese territory. He was also criticized for conducting the war from the safety of Tokyo and not basing himself in Korea. MacArthur claimed that China was fighting a total war when in fact Beijing had been very restrained, not least in using air power against front-line troops, ports or staging bases in Japan. The USSR had also committed very little of its massive firepower.

When General Ridgway replaced MacArthur he revitalized morale and organization. UN forces advanced to what was called 'Line Kansas', north of the 38th Parallel. In April 1951, in what was dubbed the Chinese Spring Offensive, approximately 700,000 northern forces advanced. The US I Corps stood firm at the Battle of Imjin River and the Battle of

Kapyong. At the end of May the US Eighth Army counter-attacked and stood once more on Line Kansas, just north of the 38th Parallel. This was a yo-yo war with a vengeance, or so it seemed then. In fact the forces were largely stalemated, exchanging very little territory.

Negotiations began in July. The war did not end, however. A series of battles ensued but with little movement as the communist forces tested the resolve of the UN to continue the fight. Negotiations continued first at Kaesong, on the ceasefire lines, and then later at nearby Panmunjom. One of the sticking points in talks was the exchange of PoWs; many communist troops as well as conscripted former Kuomintang soldiers refused to be repatriated. And the South Korean government wanted to fight on to a total victory to ensure re-unification. Nevertheless, a final armistice agreement was signed on 27 July 1953. The battle lines became the DMZ: the Demilitarized Zone.

Immediate impacts

The US suffered 33,686 killed in battle over three years, almost as many as American losses in Vietnam over *ten* years. South Korea claimed over 373,000 civilians killed and over 137,000 military fatalities. The costs to the US of the war were estimated at $30 billion. Beijing estimated that 183,000 of their military 'volunteers' had been killed. Besides many deaths, the American strategic bombing campaign and other battlefield attrition had destroyed 85 per cent of North Korea's buildings. Perhaps as many as 215,000 KPA troops were killed. It has been guesstimated that overall total battle fatalities during the three-year war amounted to 1.2 million. The DPRK had lost at least 10 per cent of its population, proportionately more than the German and Japanese losses in the Second World War. It was one of the highest rates of wartime death suffered by any country in the twentieth century.

Such a loss of life and treasure inevitably prompted much soul-searching about the lack of preparedness. Apparently, Sherman tanks from Second World War battles were reconditioned and even some museums were raided. Propeller-driven aircraft were taken from Air National Guard squadrons and rushed into front-line duties. The British found that almost half of their mortar bombs failed to work. An officer from the Gloucestershire Regiment observed after one major action with many mortar failures: 'I was surprised to see Ordnance Quality Control had already rejected them, by putting red paint along the edges of the tail-fins.' Only the US Marine Corps had kept their Second World War inventory of equipment and ammunition up to strength and in front-line condition.

At the beginning of the war the North Koreans deployed their Soviet T-34 tanks to good effect but the UN landings at Inchon cut off the KPA from its armour. Korea was poor tank country anyway, and thereafter there were no major tank battles. The UN tended to use their Shermans and M26 Pershing tanks and later the M47 Patton, along with the British Churchill, Centurion and Cromwell tanks, for infantry support and as mobile artillery.

Neither Korean state had much of a navy. After the major amphibious landing near Inchon, by and large the UN controlled the seas around the peninsula. The North Koreans did inflict some damage with magnetic mines and also occasional artillery fire from the shore.

Jet aircraft tended to dominate air combat. In the beginning the P-80 Shooting Star, first flown in 1944, was used. On 10 November 1950 Lieutenant Russell Brown, flying a Shooting Star, made history when he destroyed a Russian MiG-15 fighter in the world's first decisive all-jet combat. The Shooting Star, F9F Panther and Gloster Meteor dominated over prop-driven Soviet planes. Later, the deployment of the Chinese with the MiG-15 meant that Chinese pilots could reach and destroy the high-altitude B-29 Superfortresses even if they had fighter escort. The UN had to resort to less accurate, but safer, night bombings. The US then deployed the F-86 Sabre to try to match the very capable MiG-15. In a level dogfight, both swept-wing designs managed comparable top speeds of around 660 mph. The MiG could climb faster but the Sabre could turn and dive better.

Equally matched, the outcome of dogfights often depended on the skills and determination of the individual pilots. Moscow denied direct involvement, explaining that they provided only advisers but there were many examples of Soviet pilots speaking *en clair* in Russian in their wireless communications. The US Air Force reported that the Sabre kill rate was more than 10:1. Nearly 800 MiG–15s were shot down by Sabres, while seventy-eight Sabres were lost to enemy fire.

Besides fixed-wing aircraft, the war witnessed the extensive deployment of helicopters for medical evacuation, as the opening scene of *M*A*S*H* much later made icons of the rotary-wing aircraft. Future helicopters were to develop into an attack role, such as the AH–Cobra used extensively in the Vietnam War.

As in the Second World War, strategic bombing was a major instrument of the USAF. The Americans dropped a total of 635,000 tons of bombs on Korea, including 32,557 tons of napalm. This was more than the whole Pacific campaign of the Second World War – that is considering conventional bombs, not atomic ones. The northern forces had little anti-aircraft defence and were largely forced to move underground. The communists also claimed that the USAF had used chem-bio weapons.

In essence, Korea was a 'poor bloody infantryman's' war. Poverty, alien culture and difficult terrain made the peninsula an unwelcoming place for foreigners. As one young US soldier noted at the start of the war: 'Korea is a miserably poor, primitive, mountainous place with few paved roads or amenities …with jungles hot and steamy in the rainy season and arctic cold in winter.' And the communist troops fought well, often fanatically but they were not unbeatable. This was a similar lesson to the one the Americans and British learned fighting the Japanese.

And yet this far-off little-known poverty-stricken location came as close to nuclear confrontation as twelve years later in Cuba, a well-known country right in America's backyard.

Atomic weapons

The US Joint Chiefs of Staff issued orders on 5 November 1950 permitting the dropping of atomic bombs on Chinese military bases if regular Chinese forces invaded, or North Korean or Chinese bombers flew from China and attacked UN forces in Korea. Nine Mark 4 nuclear bombs were transferred to the USAF 9th Bomber Group, the designated carriers.

Many US military leaders then regarded A-bombs as *usable* weapons. After all, they had just been used to immediate demonstration (and explosive) effect on Japan. The deployment of nuclear-capable (but not nuclear-armed) B-29 bombers to Britain during the 1948–49 Berlin Blockade was considered a factor in getting Moscow to back down in Europe. Plans were also prepared for attacking Soviet forces if they had overtly entered the Korean War. A further deployment of B-29s was ordered to Britain – with bombs this time but not their cores. A similar deployment was ordered to Guam – and leaked to the press. As the UN forces were pinned down in the Pusan Perimeter, the CIA speculated that Beijing might have a go at overwhelming Taiwan. If that had happened there might have been real political and public pressure to use nukes to prevent a total defeat in Korea and in Taiwan, let alone in Western Europe.

President Truman said at a 30 November 1950 press conference that using atomic weapons was 'always under active consideration'. The warning seemed not to have deterred the Chinese – who for long claimed that they could survive and fight on after a nuclear assault. Egregiously, the Americans were dubbed 'paper tigers'. But America's European allies were very agitated. In early December Truman met and tried to placate both British and French premiers. They worried that an excessive focus on the Korean War, conventional or nuclear, might leave open Western Europe to a Soviet counter-strike. The Russians had tested their atomic bomb – successfully – the year before. And yet strategists still talked of fighting limited nuclear wars. The logic of MAD – mutual assured destruction – had not yet been adopted by the two superpowers. They were still 'thinking the unthinkable'.

Yet, even during the humiliating retreat to Pusan, Washington's political and diplomatic elites were never as gung-ho about using nukes as some military commanders. They were held back not least because of the fear of general war with China, or Russia. But the massive involvement of new Chinese armies either in Korea or massed near the Korean border nevertheless pushed the US further up the rungs of nuclear escalation. A-bombs were assembled at the Kadena Air Base in Okinawa and B-29s flew or practised bombing runs from Okinawa using dummy A-bombs or conventional ordnance.

It is difficult to estimate accurately the deterrence effect of the threat of limited nuclear war against China. The Americans had a small amount of A-bombs, and most of those would have been deemed necessary *in extremis* to deploy against the USSR, then considered a much bigger danger than non-nuclear Red China. It was reckoned that Moscow would not use its handful of crude atomic weapons on behalf of China or North Korea. President Dwight Eisenhower, as a former senior general, tended to be even more cautious than Truman. Despite all the nuclear sabre-rattling they were never used or even nearly used, despite some political hype at the time. The first major limited war, albeit conventional, thank God, did teach some early and important lessons about mutual deterrence.

Media perspectives

Journalists assumed that, freed from the dictates of patriotism, they could report this war with little censorship. The US military soon decided otherwise. As American correspondent Hal Boyle remarked, 'This was the worst-reported war of modern times.' Part of the reason was the actual request by some reporters for greater guidance from the military as to what they should or should not say. Some 270 correspondents were in theatre by the end of 1950, with only Wilfred Burchett and Alan Winnington covering the communist side. Most stayed at headquarters and out of the field; less than a fifth were on the front line, and many of these were Australians. The harsh terrain and weather, and the chaos of the disastrous first stage of the war, when the American-led forces were trapped in the small Pusan pocket, impelled journalists to rely on food, transport, and, above all, communications supplied by the US armed forces. All copy required routing through army headquarters in Tokyo, which resulted in numerous opportunities for selection, delay, or deliberate 'loss' of unfavourable material. Initially, however, little deliberate censorship was imposed, since most Western correspondents adhered to the propaganda line of an anti-communist crusade.

The combined Allied commander, General Douglas MacArthur, had spent two years as a press liaison officer in Washington in his early career and he had enjoyed being in the media spotlight in his glory days at the end of the Second World War. He also deployed the media for his own purposes. He even encouraged *Life* and *Newsweek* magazines to publish pictures of the bodies of soldiers who had been killed by North Korean troops. But the UN side committed atrocities too, particularly the South Koreans; and the military situation was worsening. In December 1950 MacArthur imposed strict military censorship. The voluntary 'staff officer' style of Generals Eisenhower and Montgomery was discarded. Journalists who didn't 'join the team' were ejected from theatre; seventeen suffered this fate. The new medium of television had already penetrated 65 per cent of American homes but there was no means to send the signal directly to the viewer. So censored film footage slowly reached the Stateside television audience days after events occurred.

In September 1950 MacArthur had decided to try to turn the war around with an ambitious but risky amphibious landing at Inchon. With 262 ships, it was the largest naval task force since 1945. Journalist James Cameron was in one of the assault ships with a group of other correspondents. He observed wryly that the ship had been 'full of agitated and contending correspondents, all trying to appear insistently determined to land in Wave One, while contriving desperately to be found in Wave Fifty'. After the successful landings, South Korean forces treated prisoners appallingly. Cameron, a bloodyminded and determined Scot, complained to the UN command, to no avail. Cameron reported on the atrocities and, along with photographs by Bert Hardy, sent the material to Tom Hopkinson, the editor of *Picture Post*. After much cross-checking and the inclusion of a photograph of North Korean atrocities, the story was set to be published when the proprietor of the magazine, Sir Edward Hulton, pulled it. Hopkinson protested and was fired. It became a *cause célèbre* on Fleet Street.

I.F. Stone in the USA was as determined as Cameron or Hopkinson to dissect the truth behind the official lies about the war. When his classic work *The Hidden History of the Korean War* was published, many journalists and the US government were quick to condemn it as Soviet propaganda. He had made himself almost unemployable in the era of McCarthyism, so he started the famous *I.F. Stone's Weekly*, which became a financial success and an icon of the anti-war movement in the 1960s.

Many reports about atrocities and racism in the war were hushed up, as well as many acts of military incompetence. One long-delayed story was of the amazing collapse of morale among US prisoners of war, especially compared with the successful stoicism of Turkish PoWs. Nearly every major newspaper in Britain and the United States supported the war. This was the period of Senator Joseph R. McCarthy's anti-communist witch-hunt in the United States. No one wanted to be accused of giving succour to the red peril that now consisted, it was claimed, of a monolithic communist bloc in the form of both the Soviet Union and China. After Inchon, UN forces pushed up to the Chinese border, whereupon – after many warnings – the Chinese People's Liberation Army intervened and propelled Western forces back down the peninsula. Hence the famous comment by a US Marine general: 'Retreat, hell! We're just attacking in another direction.' Another Marine told a correspondent, 'Remember, whatever you write, that this was not a retreat. All that happened was we found more Chinese behind us than in front of us. So we about-faced and attacked.'

The war ended in a negotiated stalemate in the summer of 1953. The border between North and South Korea was roughly where it had been in the summer of 1950 (and where it is today). No peace, merely an armistice, was the result. Technically, more than six decades later, a highly belligerent, and now nuclear-armed, North Korea is still at war with the South. Perhaps the intractability of the conflict explains why the shooting war came and went with much bloodshed but precious little glory and left no mark on American imaginations though nearly as many Americans died there as in Vietnam. The Korean tragedy produced few films or novels in the heroic mould. *M*A*S*H*, the most popular televised icon of the war, was actually made during the Vietnam era and bears little accurate reference to the harsh realities of the Korean situation at the time. In his account of the Korean conflict British war correspondent and historian Max Hastings concluded, 'The war seemed an unsatisfactory, inglorious, and thus unwelcome memory.'

Many Asians did not want to forget the war, however. 'Where America paid a price,' according to Henry Kissinger,

> was among revolutionary leaders of Southeast Asia and elsewhere, who discovered a method of warfare that avoided large-scale ground combat yet had the ability to wear down the resolve of a superpower.

Korea, of course, was largely a conventional war where the Western industrialized powers had a marked advantage but it spawned alternative,

Maoist-style insurgencies that played to the strengths of weaker and more patient opponents.

Unlike later in Vietnam, Britain had joined in this fight, albeit reluctantly. The British were wary of MacArthur and played a part in encouraging President Truman to fire him. They feared, rightly, that the maverick military genius was trying to incite an all-out war with China. Not for the first time, the British showed better judgement than their American allies. During the Second World War, the Americans had insisted that Chiang Kai-shek was the leader who would save China and that French military leader Charles de Gaulle was insignificant. In each case, London took the contrary view and was proved correct. Regarding Korea, Prime Minister Clement Attlee displayed good sense in helping to dissuade Truman from using nuclear weapons. The British were also more sceptical about the anti-communist ruler of South Korea, Syngman Rhee.

Legacy

The Korean conflict set the pattern for proxy wars between the superpowers until the end of the Cold War. Vietnam was the harsh result for the USA and Afghanistan helped to undermine the USSR. Other bloody examples ensued in Africa and South America.

The American empire was at the height of its power in 1950 – a little like Great Britain a century before, or Rome at its imperial zenith. Then Washington found itself committed to the most unexpected of wars in the least predicted of places – and under very unfavourable military conditions.

So many ingredients of the Korean struggle were replicated a decade later in the Indochina tragedy:

the political difficulty of sustaining an unpopular and autocratic regime; the problems of creating a credible local army in a corrupt society; the fateful costs of under-estimating the power of an Asian communist army. For all the undoubted benefits of air superiority and close support, Korea vividly displayed the difficulties of using air power effectively against a primitive economy, a peasant army.

The war also demonstrated the problem of deploying a highly mechanized Western army in broken country against a lightly equipped foe.[2]

The Vietnam tragedy was still to come. What of the immediate participants in 1953? South Korea eventually emerged from the ashes as one of the world's fastest-growing economies. In 1960 the US signed a Mutual Defense Treaty with South Korea. Originally a great deal of anti-Americanism festered in the country but later the USA became generally popular. Nearly 30,000 US troops were still stationed in the country in 2019.

Arguably, the north has never fully recovered from the war. Chinese and Soviet loans were largely cancelled and Eastern bloc aid flowed in. And yet famine and later severe food shortages continued to stalk the land – even until the time of writing. Beijing continues to support the authoritarian regime in Pyongyang despite its sometimes unruly attitude towards its main protector. The war was very expensive for the new Mao Zedong regime but it did show that, after the century of humiliation by the great powers, not least the utter humbling of the opium wars with the British, Chinese troops could stand up to Western forces and fight them to a stalemate. The many weaknesses of the People's Liberation Army were displayed, however, and Beijing started on the long road to building one of the strongest armies in the world.

Fighting in Korea had lost Beijing the key prize of Taiwan, however. In American military circles, in 1949, it was generally assumed that the communists would eventually seize the last redoubt of the Kuomintang. Yet the Korean conflict transformed the island into another domino that had to be protected by America. To this day Taiwan remains beyond the grip of Beijing. To the legacy of the civil war inside China was added the anger over the intervention in Korea and the decision to protect Taiwan – this helped to further fuel anti-Americanism in Mao's People's Republic.

Stalin's policy of re-uniting Korea had failed. And the rifts in their joint military planning were part of the reason for the souring of Sino-Soviet relations. The Russians had tested several of their new military developments, notably the MiG-15 (with its British Rolls Royce Nene-derived engine). The war, however, may have led to a more determined response to possible Soviet intervention elsewhere, such as in Yugoslavia after Marshal Tito's split with Stalin.

The North Atlantic Treaty Organization (NATO) was augmented by the inclusion of Turkey in 1952. The Turks had contributed over 5,000 able troops to front-line combat in Korea. The Australians had contributed experienced troops which led later to the ANZUS pact with Washington and New Zealand in 1951. Britain and the USA's old ally, Canada, sent almost 30,000 troops to Korea. Their naval forces had played a key role during the initial stages of the war. Most of the traditional British allies fought under the formal name of the British Commonwealth Forces Korea (BCFK), although some troops worked outside this structure under direct US or UN command. Australian troops serving in the occupation forces in Japan were among the first UN personnel to be deployed in Korea. The 1st Commonwealth Division was formed in July 1951 and British and Canadian senior officers tended to predominate in the Commonwealth land forces. Britain, after all, had rotated almost 100,000 troops, initially from the British Army of the Rhine (BAOR). Britain did have some heroic episodes but they very much played second fiddle to the US commanders. As the Second World War RAF hero, Group Captain Johnnie Johnson, noted at the time, 'I felt very much an observer of an American show.' One obvious exceptions was the Battle of Imjin River in April 1951 when 400 men from the Gloucestershire Regiment fought back over 10,000 Chinese troops. One of the 'Glorious Glosters' in the battle was Maurice Micklewhite, later to become Sir Michael Caine. British casualties in Korea were three times as many as in the solo British effort of the Falklands war.

The Royal Navy usually provided one of five Commonwealth aircraft carriers; the Australians also maintained a carrier, HMS *Sydney*. The Royal Navy also operated the only British fighter planes. On 9 August 1952 a prop-driven Sea Fury based on HMS *Ocean*, shot down a MiG-15. The pilot, Commander Peter Carmichael (inevitably nicknamed 'Hoagy'), was one of only a tiny number of pilots of piston-engined planes to shoot down a jet fighter during the Korean War. Flying his regular Hawker Sea Fury, he was leading a four-aircraft formation, when they were attacked by eight MiG-15s over North Korea. Carmichael downed the MiG with his cannon fire. It was claimed but not confirmed that a second MiG was also shot down. RAF pilots, flying on exchange with the USAF, did claim at least seven kills.

The Royal Australian Air Force flew P-51 Mustangs and, later, Gloster Meteors. No. 2 Squadron of the South African Air Force was part of the USAF's 18th Fighter-Bomber Wing, flying P-51s and F-86s.

Japan, too, was strengthened by the new alliance with the old enemy in Washington. Even a form of re-armament, in the form of the Self-Defense Forces, was permitted. Japan's rapid rise to the status of an economic superpower was partly kick-started by the Korean conflict. Another former American enemy, Germany, underwent its own *Wirtschaftswunder*; West Germany was allowed to join NATO in 1955, though it faced restrictions, not least regarding nuclear weapons.

The US itself learned from the war, after the embarrassing early setbacks. President Truman had declared a state of national emergency when it looked as though the USA, fresh from its glory days after the Second World War, was about to be defeated. The official estimates of the cost of the war amounted to perhaps $140 billion today – without counting the costs of defending the south after 1953. Not only were the forces re-equipped with new equipment, but a degree of moral re-armament was required. The way that so many US PoWs broke down and succumbed to the brainwashing disturbed Washington's military and intelligence elites – though it was generally hushed up. (So was a famous British example. George Blake, the UK's vice-consul in Seoul, was turned during his three years of North Korean captivity. The Anglo-Dutch double agent did a great deal of damage until he was arrested in 1961.[3]) One of the side-effects of the American re-organization was the integration of African-American troops. The previous world wars had fielded segregated units. By the end of 1951 US troops no longer fought in segregated units, though racism still persisted, not least in promotion opportunities.

A senior US commander said: 'We went into Korea with a very poor army and came out with a pretty good one. We went into Vietnam with a pretty good army and came out with a terrible one.'

Chapter 3

Half War/Half Peace

DMZ conflict

T he Demilitarized Zone (DMZ) runs north-east of the 38th
Parallel. The old Korean capital, Kaesong, where the original
armistice talks began, is now in North Korea, though it was
part of pre-war South Korea. The armistice agreements were signed on
27 July 1953 and the major antagonists were supposed to forge a peace
deal. It never happened. The Neutral Nations Supervisory Commission
(NNSC), composed of troops from 'neutral' states, chosen by both
Korean sides, helped to supervise the DMZ. Originally Swiss, Swedish,
Czechoslovak and Polish troops monitored in the north and south.
The collapse of the Warsaw Pact and the emancipation of Poland and
Czechoslovakia meant that they were no longer allies in Pyongyang's
eyes. After 1995 North Korea did not recognize the existence of the
NNSC. The Swedish and Swiss delegations continued to submit reports
on South Korean troop movements to Pyongyang, which were ignored.
Poland continued to attend (occasionally) NNSC meetings, although it
was no longer able to observe troop movements in North Korea.

The NNSC soon became a polite diplomatic fiction – though few
wanted actually to abolish it for fear of exacerbating tensions. Inevitably,
tens of thousands of hostile military personnel were stationed along the
highly-mined and armed DMZ. It has been far more dangerous than
the former militarized borders of the NATO vs Warsaw Pact or the
demarcation of North and South Vietnam.

The tempo of the border tension varies – sometimes local incidents
threatened to escalate into renewed war, as in 1966–69, while sometimes
extra tension is precipitated by international factors. For example, when
the North Vietnamese conquered the south of the country in 1975, the
North Korean leadership discussed with Beijing the obvious parallels

and opportunities. The Chinese Communist Party politburo refused to back another war in Korea, however. The North Koreans instead engaged in all sorts of subversion whether it was building major penetration tunnels or using submarines to torpedo South Korean vessels as well as multiple abductions of southerners. And yet, as we shall see, these were mere pinpricks compared with the threat of nuclear war once Pyongyang finally managed to cross the nuclear threshold in the twenty-first century.

The Second Korean war?

At times in the mid to late 1960s it appeared as though the Korean War was on the edge of being resumed. Russian and Chinese pressure – as well as American deterrence – played a part in preventing another conventional invasion from the north. Instead, Pyongyang engaged in irregular war. The north wanted to unify the peninsula and assumed that revolutionary tactics might inspire a rebellion in the south.

The Americans broke elements of the armistice agreement (especially paragraph 13d regarding the deployment of nuclear weapons). In January 1958 the US forces introduced nuclear-armed Honest John missiles and 280mm atomic cannon. Later, atomic demolition munitions and nuclear-armed Matador missiles were added to the inventory. Washington first deployed nuclear weapons to South Korea in 1958; numbers peaked in the late 1960s at close to 950, including a mixture of tactical and strategic weapons. North Korea asked the USSR and China for nuclear weapons of its own, or at least some help with developing them, so as to match the capitalist arsenal.

Denied atomic weapons, Kim Il-sung planned a strategy of unconventional warfare, propaganda and agit-prop in the south. Force or subversion would be required because the north increasingly failed to attract any economic envy in the south. The DPRK remained mired in poverty while gradually South Korea underwent a West German-style economic miracle. Economic growth under the protection of the American nuclear umbrella gave the south extra confidence, not least that the north would not – or could not – overwhelm the south again. The confidence even allowed Seoul to send numerous and often elite troops to aid the US in Vietnam in 1965.

The conventional military option would still reinforce the north's irregular strategy. The Korean People's Army deployed eight infantry divisions along the DMZ. The unconventional strategy was centred on the Reconnaissance Bureau of the Ministry of Defense. This bureau comprised special forces that were highly trained in demolition, subversion and small-unit combat tactics. The SF were called simply the 124th and 283rd army units; each unit numbered about 1,000 men, all officers. The Reconnaissance Bureau also ran 23 Amphibious Brigade that specialized in infiltration along the South Korean coastline, twenty-eight times longer than the DMZ. Besides these regular special forces, North Korea deployed thousands of 'civilian' agents in the south.

American and South Korean forces under US control in the UN Command (Korea) were prepared for possible major incursions but the growing demands for troops in Vietnam depleted both armies' manpower. The best equipment went to Vietnam too; only twelve Huey choppers were available at one stage to hunt for possible infiltrators. The better trained and motivated American officers and NCOs preferred to see action in Vietnam. Lack of men, equipment and motivation undermined the counter-insurgency effort. No specialist COIN units or strategic co-ordination existed when the DMZ crisis flared up in 1966. US intelligence also winked at a number of South Korean sabotage ops in North Korea.

North Korea started to increase penetration of agents in 1964. By 1966 South Korean clashes with northern agents were rapidly growing. The north, however, initially avoided action along the US-controlled parts of the DMZ. In October 1966 the South Koreans staged a major retaliatory raid into the north without seeking the approval of the US commander of the joint forces, General Charles H. Bonesteel III. The general came from a distinguished military family, four generations of West Pointers, and had served in the Second World War, Korea and Vietnam. Notable for his eyepatch and nickname 'Tick', Bonesteel was an intellectual, not a back-slapping Patton. The former Rhodes Scholar at Oxford had seen very little combat and was not a soldier's soldier but he was a good diplomat. He had to be – he was wearing various hats as US and UN commander as well as chief liaison officer with the South Korean military. Unlike the US role in NATO or General William Westmoreland in Vietnam, the senior American general in South Korea directed the coalition of forces.

This meant three jobs had to be done by Bonesteel, but it also ensured the silver lining of unity of command, though not always of strategic intent. The Americans wanted to preserve the status quo and to avoid another major peninsular war. The South Korean top brass, however, wanted unification, probably by force. In 1945 Bonesteel had helped to draw up the 38th Parallel as the 'temporary' division. And the general worked hard to avoid any obvious violations of the armistice turning into a Korean War Mark 2.

Then, in November 1966, regular KPA forces attacked US troops. General Bonesteel needed to find a counter strategy, and urgently. The US training manuals did not have a suitable COIN doctrine that could deal with conventional and irregular tactics. Bonesteel defined three types of operations:

- Direct infiltration across the DMZ
- Naval operations along the coast
- Counter-insurgency ops in the interior

All had to work, while maintaining conventional deterrence, and thus avoiding all-out conventional war, even more dangerous since Beijing had become a nuclear power in 1964.

The armistice agreement restricted heavy weapons in the DMZ. Defences were supposed to be limited to patrols and observation posts. Patrols were made more regularly and more aggressively, and ambushes were set up at night. Most US casualties resulted from these patrols. The observation posts were fortified and machine guns and recoilless rifles were hidden because they breached the armistice. Beyond the southern boundary of the DMZ (usually called the 'south tape') no defensive restrictions applied. Three-metre-tall chain-link fences topped with concertina wire, and behind it a raked-sand path, were set up; next came minefields and more barbed wire, plus machine guns and mortars and artillery. Fortified observation towers were erected plus electronic sensors, similar to the so-called McNamara Line in Vietnam. Mostly these barriers were ineffective against determined and well-trained infiltrators – the North Koreans could get through the fence in under a minute with the right tools and propitious circumstances. But the barriers slowed infiltrators to some extent and often enabled quick-reaction forces the extra time to hunt them down. The US rules of engagement were eased to allow artillery fire against known KPA positions in the north – though this tactic was used sparingly. Under Bonesteel, the big artillery and heavy mortars were used only three times. 'I wasn't much for body counts,' said the commanding general, in reference to the obsession with counting enemy deaths in Vietnam. The South Koreans were, however, more active in cross-border raids – sometimes using small teams of turned KPA defectors.

The southern navy, with just seventy-two ships, found it hard to monitor the nearly 7,000 kilometres of rugged island-strewn coast line. Poor communications, few rapid-reaction forces, and lack of helicopters meant that successful amphibious DRPK landings at night were common. Bonesteel said: 'When I got here in September 1966 there were only four or five Hueys. That was the *total* number of Hueys in South Korea.'

The Americans regarded counter-insurgency as a domestic matter, although General Bonesteel did assist with SF training and use of helicopters, once the number was increased. Initially Bonesteel had no SF Green Berets to call on. Later, however, calling on the 1st SF group in Okinawa, Bonesteel did send some Green Berets into the Taebaek and southern Chiri mountains. The internal insurgency problems were largely dealt with on an ad hoc basis by the ROK army, police and the Korean Central Intelligence Agency.

Park Chung-hee, the third South Korean president, was reluctant to arm civilian militias as he feared insurrection against his rule. President Park was a powerful figure – he ruled from 1963 to 1979 when he was assassinated. Obsessed since childhood by the legacy of Napoleon, whom he tried to emulate, he had served in the Imperial Japanese Army and then rose rapidly in the (Republic of Korea Army) ROKA. At the expense of civil rights, as president he played a big part in the economic miracle. His rule was sometimes dubbed 'developmental dictatorship'.

Despite President Park's passion for military affairs he was slow to construct a proper co-ordinated COIN system. But by late 1967 it became evident that the North Koreans were attempting to generate a full-blown insurgency in the south, with 'liberated areas' in the Taebaek mountains. President Park now worked closely with Bonesteel to establish a national co-ordinating strategy with a formal chain of command to deal with a spectrum ranging from individual agents to widespread insurgency. Ten new ROKA COIN battalions were formed, along with the expansion of the Combat Police. Eventually, the Homeland Defense Reserve Force (HDRF), comprising two million volunteers, was formed.

COIN balance of power

Kim Il-sung had been trained in conventional Soviet doctrine but his own experience of guerrilla warfare against the Japanese had influenced his shift to a new strategy. And, also, as Pyongyang's entente with Moscow waned, the need to embrace China's brand of Maoist insurgency increased proportionately. Initially, the northern army did not have formal political officers. The regular officers had rather more initiative than was normal in communist armies. The KPA was well trained, experienced and committed. When cornered, infiltrators would often prefer death by hand-grenade rather than surrender. Man-for-man North Korean special forces were possibly the toughest soldiers the Americans had ever encountered, perhaps including even German SS troops in Normandy.

The north infiltrated all year but there were campaign seasons. The communist special forces preferred the dry ground, longer nights and fogs of early autumn – before the snows came; unlike in the spring the summer vegetation was still sufficient to shield their movements; September, October and the first two weeks of November became the prime infiltration times. Even the hardiest northern SF units tended to avoid the bitterly cold Korean winters, as they would be on foot. So the insurgency fighting season was usually March to November.

As both sides found in 1950–53, the terrain and weather suited the defender who was prepared. And the south had been preparing for over a decade. If the climate and terrain could benefit the conventional defence, it could also help infiltrators – or 'leakers' as they were dubbed.

Cultural factors were obviously as crucial as topography. The Koreans were one of the most homogenous cultures and peoples in the world. Yet it was not that simple. The northern infiltrators could often relate well to the southern peasants who were technically classic fodder for Maoist indoctrination. The SF infiltrators or locally-based agents could appeal to a common heritage and the Koreans' instinctive dislike of foreign overlords, whether Japanese or American. Southerners, however, could also point to the northerners' embrace of both the Russians and Chinese. In addition, southerners had always regarded the northerners as crude and aggressive compared with the more refined people in the south. And the savage behaviour of the invading communist armies had added to the northern reputation for aggression.

The southern farmers were perhaps less inclined to embrace Kim Il-sung's version of Maoism for a number of reasons. Firstly, it would be wrong to underestimate the impact of the new but sometimes persuasive brand of South Korean nationalism. Very many farmers, perhaps the majority, had benefitted from the recent land reforms that had given them ownership of the land they had worked on previously as tenants. It was one thing for northern agit-prop to trumpet that the farmers had sold out to capitalist gold but new affluence was an important factor for stabilization. The southern miracle was soon to cement many undecided rural poor into the Republic of Korea's future prosperity.

In the balance of power, the Americans held many of the top cards. Nuclear deterrence and Chinese and Russian constraints as well as the increasing firepower of the ROKA were likely to deter another big invasion. The north had to strike quickly, probably with a big land push after a blitzkrieg air strike in the style of the Israelis in 1967 against their Arab enemies. Normally time favours insurgents, especially patient ones influenced by Mao. And yet the north needed quick results before the rapid growth of not only the South Korean economy but also Seoul's new diplomatic alliances in Asia, especially with Japan, turned the south into a state strong enough to survive alongside its superpower benefactor. Provided the Americans held their nerve and avoided all-out war, the south would win, almost by default.

Holding one's nerve usually depended on leadership in any war, especially COIN. Bonesteel was an excellent commander but many of his men were of poor quality. US troops came and went individually, usually serving for thirteen months, one month longer than the tours in Vietnam. Bonesteel could sometimes keep people a little longer, maybe two months' extension, and a few keen officers might stay even longer. But many of the ordinary soldiers were of poor quality from the so-called 'Project 100,000' that swept up disadvantaged and uneducated conscripts who became unruly and unhappy soldiers. And they needed a lot more training by good NCOs who were in short supply anyway. Weak leadership in the junior officer ranks as well the short tours and priority of Vietnam all added to Bonesteel's difficulties.

ROKA army conscripts, however, were drafted for thirty-six months and the rank and file were usually of good quality with an impressive esprit de corps. Often their sound morale and fighting spirit made up for their lack of modern weapons and air mobility.

Major incidents

Blue House attack

It was the night of 17 January 1968 when thirty-one highly trained North Korean operatives, called Unit 124, were ordered 'to go to Seoul and cut off the head of Park Chung-hee'. The northern planners assumed that the assassination of President Park would be the key to getting the oppressed southerners to rise up against their American overlords and South Korean puppets. Unit 124 operatives entered Seoul in small groups of two to three men. They liaised in a safe house and donned ROKA uniforms and started to march to the Blue House (the presidential palace, in fact a compound of traditional houses). Their cover was that they were a COIN patrol to stop the rumoured infiltration of the capital. They got to within 800 metres of the palace when they were stopped by a suspicious police unit. A big gun battle ensued. Survivors of the fighting tried to escape and re-cross the DMZ. Nearly all of the thirty-one-man Unit 124 were killed or captured in the ensuing manhunt; only one managed to get back to the north.

The Pueblo Incident

A number of specific Korean and Asia-wide crises happened at the same time. In January 1968 a US Navy 'spy ship', the USS *Pueblo*, and its crew were seized by the North Koreans. In the same month the North Koreans staged a major assassination attempt on the southern president in his own home. The period also marked the beginning of the Tet Offensive in South Vietnam. Although the offensive was defeated, and it was a technical victory for American-led COIN forces, it was a *political* disaster for the Western superpower. It became clear that the West had not won the war; to the contrary, the powerful TV pictures of the fighting suggested an imminent North Vietnamese victory. It was not surprising that the Kim Il-sung regime should try to press its geo-political advantage.

On 5 January 1968 the USS *Pueblo* left the US naval base of Yokosuka in Japan and sailed to another base at Sasebo, also in Japan. On 11 January the ship headed through the Tsushima Strait into the Sea of Japan. The spy ship, which had been commissioned in 1945, was gathering intelligence on Soviet naval activity in the Tsushima Strait and also harvesting signal intelligence from North Korea. The ship's orders were to transit down the North Korean coast but not to get closer than thirteen nautical miles from the coast line. The captain, Commander Lloyd M. 'Pete' Bucher, later admitted that 'I did not have a highly professional group of seamen to do my navigational chores for me.'

Not only did the crew lack the requisite skills but no one had told the captain that a major assassination attempt had been made on the Blue House. He needed to be on high alert and especially not to sail too near North Korean territorial waters. Instead he was on a solo mission, without any back-up. Bucher's commanding officer had told him 'to avoid another Korean war'.

In the early evening of 23 January 1968 a North Korean modified SO-1-class Russian submarine-chaser passed close by the US ship. The Americans reckoned they were 15.4 nautical miles off the coast. Then two North Korean fishing trawlers also sailed very close to the *Pueblo*. The submarine-chaser ordered the *Pueblo* to stand down or be fired upon. The American vessel tried to manoeuvre away but it was considerably slower than the North Korean gunship. The *Pueblo* was an antiquated former army cargo freighter with a top speed of just 13 knots and its armaments were two jamming-prone .50 calibre machine guns. Several warning shots were fired by the North Koreans. Three North Korean torpedo boats joined in the fray; two MiG-21 fighters appeared and then a fourth torpedo boat and another submarine chaser. The *Pueblo*'s machine guns were wrapped in cold-weather tarpaulins and the ammunition was stored below decks. Worse, only one member of the crew had proper experience with the guns. No attempt was made to man the guns. It would have been suicidal to attempt to ready the weapons in the face of vastly superior and adjacent North Korean firepower.

Whether the *Pueblo* entered North Korean waters is something of a moot point. Washington claimed that their ship remained outside the standard twelve-nautical-mile limit but Pyongyang argued that their waters extended to fifty miles.

One of the submarine-chaser vessels opened fire with a 57mm cannon and some of the smaller vessels raked the US ship with machine-gun fire – after it had tried to manoeuvre away from the North Korean attempts to board her. One crew member of the *Pueblo* was killed.

The US crew had very little time to destroy a massive hoard of classified material on the ship which later gave the North Koreans a wealth of intelligence. The US Seventh Fleet was aware of the *Pueblo*'s plight but the promised air cover did not arrive. The USAF had no aircraft on strip-alert in the vicinity. The *Pueblo* followed the escorting ships but then stopped at the twelve-mile limit. The North Koreans started firing again, killing an American sailor. Ten were wounded, including the captain. The *Pueblo* was finally boarded; the crew were handcuffed, blindfolded and beaten.

Once the story broke, US Congressman Mendel Rivers told President L.B. Johnson that he should threaten a nuclear response if the captured ship and crew were not returned. More cautious US politicians advocated restraint, not least because they feared the crew might be killed.

Military readiness of US forces was dramatically stepped up in the region. The top brass considered a naval blockade of North Korean ports. Washington even started talking to the Russians, because it was assumed that Moscow had a guiding hand in the crisis. Later, when secret files where opened after the end of the (first) Cold War, it appeared likely that the North Koreans acted opportunistically and largely alone and that their bravado had antagonized the usually cautious Soviet politburo. Pyongyang did not share with the Russians any information about the later negotiations with the Americans concerning the release of the crew. The Chinese were kept informed, however, and may even have been instrumental in pushing the Americans to the brink. The Russians, though, made it clear that, despite their defence treaty with North Korea and China, Moscow would not go to war with the Americans on either ally's behalf.

The *Pueblo* was anchored in Wonsan, and later moved to the Botong river in Pyongyang as a prize exhibit in the Fatherland Liberation War Museum. It remains the second oldest commissioned ship in the US Navy[1] and also one of the few ships of the US Navy to have been captured since the naval wars against pirates off the Barbary Coast at the start of the nineteenth century. The crew members were starved and regularly tortured. Commander Bucher was put through a mock firing squad and then threatened with witnessing his crew being shot in front of him if he did not 'confess'. He duly wrote a confession.

The CIA went into overdrive to investigate Bucher's past, especially his Dickensian upbringing as an orphan, initially to see if he had a predilection for communism. Then they feared he had been blackmailed by communist agents. Apart from a few dalliances with Japanese bar girls, Captain Bucher had been an exemplary officer, serving first on submarines and then on surface spying missions. Moreover, he had shown stupendous bravery and leadership during his imprisonment. Although he lost half his body weight, he still risked a hunger strike in protest at the treatment of his men.

At the ensuing negotiations at Panmunjom, the North Koreans played ultra-hardball. Following a written apology and an admission that the US Navy had been spying and also promised that Washington would not spy in the future, the eighty-two surviving crew members were released. Two days before Christmas 1968, the crew was bussed to the DMZ and walked in single file, led by Bucher, across the so-called 'Bridge of No Return', eleven months after their capture.

The officers and crew appeared before a US Navy Court of Enquiry. Captain Bucher and some of his officers faced a court martial for surrendering without a fight, the first time this had happened since 1807. They were also charged with failing to destroy a wealth of classified information. Eventually it was decided that they had suffered enough and the political decision was made that no charges were to be brought. It was clear that the *Pueblo* captain had originally been fingered to be a scapegoat for the Navy's failings in not providing back-up or even the rapid means to destroy the secret documents quickly.[2] One of the reasons Bucher had stalled and tried manoeuvring for an extra two hours was to give time for the crew to get rid of some of the sensitive equipment and documents. According to a recent analysis, the material did not significantly undermine the American military effort, although the capture of the ship and her eavesdropping gear was called at the time one of the 'worst intelligence debacles in US history'. Of the 539 classified documents and pieces of equipment on board the ship, up to 80 per cent had been compromised, according to the immediate intelligence assessment. Only 5 per cent of the electronic gear had been 'destroyed beyond repair or usefulness'. Senior military intelligence officials worried that the North Vietnamese, in particular, might tighten their communications security, making their secret messages harder to crack and putting US forces in greater danger. The Soviets also reverse-engineered the communications devices on the *Pueblo* and so they made some gains despite their disapproval of the capture. Declassified Soviet archives later revealed that Moscow was very concerned to rein in Kim Il-sung's adventurism, though Moscow continued to help subsidise the regime.

Winding down the Korean War Mark 2

The immediate consensus in Washington's intelligence circles in the beginning of 1968 was that of a general communist conspiracy: that the seizure of the *Pueblo* and attacks on the Blue House were to distract US attention from Vietnam and encourage South Korean troops to be returned home. The purpose of these incidents was to divert attention from the situation in Vietnam. That was President Johnson's opinion. In Seoul, however, General Bonesteel regarded the *Pueblo* episode as merely North Korean opportunism and the timing of the Tet Offensive was coincidental, not part of an integrated Red conspiracy.

Pyongyang was always trying to split the alliance between Seoul and the US military. The Blue House raid and the *Pueblo* debacle fired up the 'Go North' hardline military policy of some of those in the Park regime in Seoul. President Park regarded the negotiations between the US and the North Koreans at Panmunjom to secure the release of the *Pueblo*'s crew as appeasement. Relations were distinctly chilly between the team of General Bonesteel and the US ambassador, William J. Porter, and, on the other side, Park.

In February 1968 President Johnson sent a personal representative, Cyrus Vance, the former deputy secretary of defense, to see President Park. There would be no return to widescale war, Vance repeated forcibly. Any ROK troops engaging in cross-border operations would have to get firstly the approval of General Bonesteel and then the direct permission of the US president. And it was up to Washington how to negotiate the release of the *Pueblo* crew. President Park concurred once he was bribed with more US military aid (especially the F-4D Phantom II fighters).

In short, Washington would not allow the South Koreans 'to go north'.

After the *Pueblo*, the stationing of so many planes and ships, and extra men in the Operations FORMATION STAR and COMBAT FOX had deterred North Korean adventurism. The ROK army was beefed up with new training and material. The DMZ was fitted out with new anti-infiltration defences. The number of Hueys was doubled to support counter-infiltration. Dog-tracker teams were also set up. The few precious M-16 automatic rifles were introduced. This gave the ROKA the firepower to equal the PPSh sub-machine guns and the AK-47 assault rifles. Finally, the government set up the Homeland Defense Reserve Force (HDRF) which incorporated over two million volunteers in 60,000 local defence units. The country already had tens of thousands of 'watchers', unarmed observers, to monitor the coasts. But when they had spotted something previously the regular rapid-action units rarely got there in time. Civic action and medical units were sent into remote areas, especially in the mountainous Taebaek and Chiri areas. Clinics and classrooms were built. New roads were constructed and wells were dug. In short, COIN was taken seriously, not least in equipment, manpower and co-ordination.

Despite this intense effort, it was still not possible to quarantine the whole coast line. Right at the start, in late 1966, in a series of incidents a KPN midget submarine had been flushed out in the Imjin estuary by the South Korean navy, and spy boats continued to raid or covertly land agents. Then, on the night of 30 October 1968, around 120 special forces from North Korea landed at eight separate locations in Gangwon province. They moved inland to create guerrilla bases in the Taebaek

Mountains. ROK forces were rapidly flown in via some of the new Hueys recently provided. Other COIN units soon joined the man hunt and within two weeks most of the North Korean infiltrators had been killed or captured. The ROK now knew what to do and the Americans knew how to help them without doing it for them.

This was the last spasm of the north's insurgency effort. The south had failed to rise up. And the US-South Korean alliance was arguably stronger than before. President Park's authoritarian approach had won general support in the south because his iron-man strategy had deterred the north. Kim Il-sung purged the senior military leaders who had co-ordinated the two-year insurgency. Some were imprisoned while others, including the defence minister, General Kim Chongbong, were executed. Some of the special infiltration units were disbanded or merged with conventional forces. North Korea had changed course in its strategy but that did not mean that all infiltrations and subversion ended.

On Kim Il-sung's birthday, 15 April 1969, two MiGs shot down a US Navy Lockheed Warning Star aircraft on an electronic intelligence mission over 160 kilometres off the coast of North Korea, killing thirty-one crewmen. President Richard Nixon and National Security Adviser Henry Kissinger first considered a retaliatory air strike. Fully engaged in Vietnam, the White House eventually backed down, fearing a return to full-scale war. A protest was lodged and accepted by the North Koreans at Panmunjom. And the USAF returned to the policy of ensuring that future intelligence flights would have proper fighter escorts. And, in late April, the Seventh Fleet's Task Force – including four carriers – conducted major operations off the coast of North Korea.

After this show of force, and the change in northern strategy, it was clear that Pyongyang had given up on its policy of an insurgency leading to the overthrow of the Park government. The US began to reduce troop numbers in the south. This was part of the Nixon doctrine that encouraged America's allies to defend themselves with US air (and nuclear) support but they had to provide the bulk of ground troops themselves. While aimed primarily at South Vietnam, it also applied to South Korea.

In October 1969 Bonesteel handed over command of US forces in Korea to General John H. Michaelis. He had had a 'good' war in Europe, and had been an inspiring fighting commander in the worst initial days of the (first) Korean War. One of the new commander's first tasks was to negotiate the release of three American soldiers captured when their OH-23 helicopter was shot down after straying across the DMZ. Their release on 3 December marked the end of the 1966–69 period of major north-south hostility.[3]

US forces had suffered 34,000 killed in battle in the 1950–53 war. In the 'second war', the southern allies had lost 1,120 soldiers and police killed. The US Army in South Korea – mainly second-rate – had improved under General Bonesteel's command. After 1970 the size of the US force was reduced and the Vietnam problems – drugs, poor race relations and indiscipline – spread to American troops in South Korea. Unlike Westmoreland in Vietnam, Bonesteel did not have to report to the US ambassador in Seoul on operational matters. Bonesteel co-ordinated with the South Korean president but he had effective operational control of both US and South Korean armies. (The US Navy helped a little and the USAF was occasionally more supportive during crises.) In his main strategic endeavour, however, Bonesteel achieved his goal. He avoided escalation to a mid-intensity or high-intensity war. 'One Asian war was enough,' Bonesteel said. 'I was trying to maintain the peace. So we wouldn't have to fight another one.' In the late 1960s America was engulfed by race riots and student protests, not least about 'crazy Asian wars'. South Vietnam was slipping from US control; South Korea, however, stayed within the US orbit. Economically it prospered, as the strength of Samsung and Hyundai were later to testify, though the COIN strategy in the country's interior was to reinforce the overbearing military in Seoul. Both were legacies of the second war.

Chapter 4

The Leadership

Kim Il-sung (1948–94)
Kim Jong-il (1994–2011)
Kim Jong-un (2011–present)

N orth Korean history resembles 'a particularly gruesome
season of *Game of Thrones* crossed with the writings of L. Ron
Hubbard, only much stranger'.[1]

On the surface three generations of the same family have ruled the
hermit kingdom but the official hagiographies are based on half-concealed
stories of assassinations, infanticides, exile and poisoning. It was never a
loving family. The story is somewhat like *Macbeth* but with nukes.

The Great Dictator

Kim Il-sung was one of the longest-ruling leaders of the twentieth century.
He outlived his mentors: Stalin by four decades and Mao by almost two
decades. He was not the automatic choice of leader of the country when
the Russians took over in the immediate post-war period but he became
the head of the Workers' Party of Korea and then effectively head of state
from 1948 to his death in 1994. He created an utterly dirigiste state that
came to almost totally control the lives of its citizens. That state was later
regulated by the philosophy of *Juche*: a form of Marxism-Leninism with
elements of Maoism but also attuned to Korean nationalism, socialism
and, above all, an almost paranoid self-reliance. And yet paradoxically
North Korea became heavily dependent upon subsidies from the Soviet
bloc and later on from Beijing (and most ironically from South Korea
and the USA). While the two communist giants were in loose alliance
that could work; when the USSR and the People's Republic of China
eventually came to blows – literally – then North Korea was caught

between them. And when the Soviet Union collapsed and aid dried up, North Korea suffered shocking levels of famine. Gradually, Pyongyang came to rely diplomatically almost exclusively – though petulantly – upon the Chinese Big Brother.

When Kim Il-sung came to power, the road to socialist achievement via self-reliance, plus a little help from your friends, looked plausible. It could be argued that the north overtook the south, briefly, in the chaotic years after the first Korean War. In the early days of his rule Kim Il-sung was genuinely popular, not least because of his reputation as a fighter against the Japanese and then the American imperialists. Yes, the state hagiographies and propaganda churned out endless praise of the 'Great Leader' but that does not entirely dismiss the original grounds for popularity. Even Japanese sources confirmed his status as a tough and efficient guerrilla commander. Few leaders have shaped their countries as much as Kim Il-sung. Kemal Atatürk and Mao may perhaps stand comparison, except that the Turkish nation-builder could not erase the hold of Islam over his people and much of the Chinese leader's legacy was soon rejected or ignored after his death.

Rise of the Great Leader

Kim Song-ju was born (probably) in a small village near Pyongyang in 1912, on 15 April, the same day as the *Titanic* sank. His family, largely Presbyterian, was forced to flee to Manchuria, perhaps because of its anti-Japanese views. Savage Japanese repression of any opposition, religious or political, as well as food shortages, forced many Korean families to flee north. The young Kim flirted with Marxism; he was jailed briefly for pro-communist subversion. In 1931 Kim joined the Chinese communist party (because the communist party of Korea, founded in 1925, was considered to be too nationalist and was thrown out of the Communist International). Kim was notably anti-Japanese – even though the imperial forces did not invade Manchuria until the end of 1931. In 1935 he joined a guerrilla band under the aegis of the Chinese communists. Kim worked first as a political commissar and then as a commander of around 160 soldiers. In the same year he assumed the nom de guerre of 'Kim Il-sung' which roughly translates as 'Kim becomes the sun'. In June 1937 he led a few hundred men to capture a small Japanese-held town of Pochonbo just over the heavily protected border in Korea. Even though the so-called 'Kim Division' held the town for just a few hours, it was considered a major political success for the Chinese communists who were battling against both local nationalist and foreign forces. Strategically, the Korean guerrilla attacks on the Japanese imperialists were little more than a nuisance, however.

Nevertheless, the Japanese did take Kim seriously and called him 'The Tiger' on their wanted lists. And they did set up a special unit to hunt him down; for 110 days in the winter of 1937–38 Kim's men evaded the Japanese pursuers in what became known as the 'Arduous March'. Interestingly, the Japanese special unit included a number of Korean soldiers who were later to hold important posts in the South Korean military during the 1950–53 war. North Korean hagiography has Kim Il-sung fighting in the mountains of North Korea with his base at the sacred Mount Paektu. In fact from 1940 to 1945 he was based just outside the Soviet Siberian city of Khabarovsk.

In 1940, according to North Korean sources, Kim's first wife was captured and was killed by the Japanese when Kim refused to surrender in exchange for her life. By the end of 1940 the Korean 'division' had been hammered by the imperial Japanese forces and Kim led his surviving men into the Soviet Union by crossing the Amur river. Kim's troops were re-trained and then assigned to the 88th Special Reconnaissance Brigade as part of the Soviet Twenty-fifth Army made up of Chinese and Korean soldiers who had fought as guerrillas in Manchuria. Promoted to major, Kim served with distinction until the end of the Second World War. The small group of officers who worked with Kim were nearly all poorly educated rural-based hesitance fighters who had lived just over the borders of their homeland, most of whom had never been to a Korean city but they came to entirely dominate the future DPRK.

Kim was handpicked by Stalin's secret police chief, Lavrentiy Beria, to become a leader of pro-Soviet forces in Korea. After twenty-six years of exile, Kim returned on 19 September 1945 to the port of Wonsan. His secret police minders had to coach him, not least in how to deliver a speech in Korean. He had only eight years of formal education, in Chinese, and then military training in Russian. Wearing a borrowed suit a size or two too small for him, along with his medals, he read out a turgid speech – 'like a duck quacking', according to a hostile witness. Frank Dikötter's 2019 book, *How to be a Dictator*, said that Kim looked like 'a delivery-boy from a Chinese eatery'.

Because Kim had learned to drink like Soviet officers, plus his ability to procure attractive women and the fact that he was more pliant than his main rivals, the local Soviet top brass backed him. At the end of 1945 Kim became chairman of the North Korean branch of the Korean communist party. Kim was not the first choice to become the front man of the Soviets' popular front government in Pyongyang. The Soviet military leadership in North Korea, however, backed a man well versed in the ways of the Red Army. And Moscow's men helped Kim forge the Korean People's Army (KPA) with the leadership core of Koreans who had fought the Japanese and the Chinese nationalist forces. Stalin also permitted the arming of the KPA with relatively modern Soviet equipment.

The USSR recognized Kim's government as sovereign in the whole peninsula, including the south. The country's division, therefore, was ideologically merely a temporary blip in the march of socialist progress. Land was redistributed and heavy industry was nationalized. The north had most of the industry, while the south possessed the best arable land. Healthcare was also taken over by the state and made free. In recognition of the munificence of the Great Leader, statues and pictures of Kim started to appear everywhere. Soon a cult grew that dwarfed even the slavish devotion to Stalin in the USSR. The calendar in the DPRK starts in 1912, the year the 'Eternal President' was born.

The Korean War entrenched Kim's position as dictator but only in some respects. Kim had pushed for the invasion and the main allies were cautious. Both the USSR and China were sucked in more and more, and Kim came to resent Beijing's military dominance in the direction of the war. Despite the 1953 stalemate, Kim proclaimed the war to be a victory. It is true that he had remained in power, a victory of sorts, but his country's infrastructure had been destroyed. To rebuild, Kim ordered a total command economy of production in agriculture and industry. While leaning towards Beijing in the deepening Sino-Soviet rift, Chairman Kim was still indebted to Beijing and was not master of his own fate in his own country until the last Chinese troops left in October 1958. Kim continued purges of both pro-Moscow and pro-Chinese elements in his own party. Public executions and mass imprisonments followed as North Korea inaugurated the *songbun* structure. This augmented a traditional caste system even more rigid than the Indian version in the days of the Raj. North Koreans were divided into core, wavering and hostile classes. Everything then followed: food rationing, jobs, accommodation and location. Those who had been considered collaborators with the Japanese, or South Koreans, intellectuals, Christians, former landowners and any vaguely oppositionist types, if they were not executed or put in camps, were sent to the country's impoverished northern provinces, usually with the poorest soil. So when the great famines came, their families often starved to death.

Kim worked hard on his balancing act between Moscow and Beijing, though the general trajectory was more pro-Chinese – partly interrupted by Kim's concern about the instability caused by the Cultural Revolution. At the same time Kim flirted with eastern bloc countries, especially the German Democratic Republic and Romania. Bucharest's drive for self-sufficiency and the personality cult around Nicolae Ceauşescu mirrored some of Kim's dictatorial preferences. Ho Chi Minh's determination to unite Vietnam also attracted the admiration of Kim. The North Vietnamese example partly inspired North Korea's insurgency operations against the south in the period 1966–69. Ho Chi Minh succeeded; Kim failed.

Kim revamped his million-strong army and continued to abduct tens of thousands of South Koreans, Japanese and even Chinese to supplement deficiencies in his professional classes. Kim also changed the constitution to make himself president in 1972. What mattered to Kim was control of the army – generals were imprisoned or executed, especially after the perceived failures of the 'Second Korean War'.

What also mattered to President Kim was who would succeed him. In 1980 it was announced that Kim's son, Kim Jong-il, would take over. This was the first patrifilial succession in communist history. And it would come at a very difficult time. *Juche* had not helped the economy. The collapse of the Soviet Union and the end of the Warsaw Pact denied Pyongyang its major Western allies. Gradually, the Great Leader handed over key institutions, especially the chairmanship of the National Defence

Commission, responsible for the control of the armed forces, to his heir apparent. President Kim also began the uranium enrichment process, allegedly for purely energy proposes.

Towards the end of his regime he had been lionized to such an extent that Leonardo da Vinci would have been jealous of this Korean polymath. He was the country's leading novelist, its top literary critic as well as historian plus a military genius and champion tennis player; he was a revered architect, industrial management specialist and agriculturalist to name just a few of his skills. He was also a heavy smoker and the very large non-malignant tumour on his neck forced photographers to take pictures from just one angle. On 8 July 1994 Kim Il-sung died from a heart attack. 'The Great Heart has stopped beating' – the official verdict of regime propaganda. The country built around a personality cult had lost its personality. Like Lenin, his embalmed body was placed in a glass coffin in a public mausoleum. Despite his death, he still remains the country's 'eternal' president, general secretary of the ruling party and various other titles. Even in death the cult survived for the 'Eternal Leader'. His birthday, the 'Day of the Sun', is still celebrated every year as a public holiday. He left a 100-volume collection of collected works and an eight-volume autobiography as well as many plays and operas – according to the Pyongyang government. By his interminable writings he added boredom to his long list of atrocities.

His main legacy, however, is the survival of his deadly Orwellian state run by three generations of his family.

Kim Jong-il – The Dear Leader

Kim Il-Sung's son was born in Vyatskoye, then part of USSR, in 1941 (although the official hagiographies claim he was born in a secret military camp on the sacred Paektu mountain in Korea, a year later). By the early 1980s – a decade before the Great Leader's death – the younger Kim was made the successor and given key posts in the army and party. He became the commander of the world's fourth-largest standing army.

Kim Jong-il had returned to Korea with his father in 1945, though where he was educated as a boy is disputed. Official sources say in Korea, although he may well have been moved to the security of China during the Korean War.

Some sources alleged that, aged around six, Kim Jong-il drowned his younger brother (Kim Man-il), by repeatedly dunking him underwater while playing in a pond. Kim Jong-il may also have received some English-language education during his occasional visits to Malta. Although Kim Il-sung had another son who had served as an ambassador to Poland, it was Kim Jong-il who was anointed as the successor at the Sixth Party Congress in October 1980. Until then he had received very little political publicity. Kim Jong-il hardly ever spoke in public – he was somewhat reclusive, unlike his gregarious father. Without any military background, the second Kim could not bask in the military glory that had accrued to the founding father of the state. The dictator's son was 'a film lover, a heavy-drinking playboy with a bouffant hairdo whose main contribution to the state was the movies he directed'.[2]

Nevertheless, the state began building a 'Dear Leader' cult around him. In 1992 radio broadcasts started referring to him as 'Dear Father' and massive celebrations were held for his fiftieth birthday. Despite his lack of military background, or any real training in other skills, the new leader began to exert even more control, sometimes even micro-managing affairs such as the size and furnishing of accommodation for senior cadres.

When his father died aged 82 on 8 July 1994, the heir, aged 52, took over but it has been suggested by defectors – often the main source of information on the most closed of all political systems – that he took some time to consolidate his absolute position, partly because of his apparent reputation of total incompetence in economic matters. He was always coming up with crazy schemes, not least to counter the famines. For example, he advocated nationwide ostrich farms to feed his people. Like the bird, that also did not fly. Only 18 per cent of the country was arable, industry was very backward and foreign aid had dried up. The government policy of 'military first' created the extensive famines when Kim Jong-il took over. So bad was the famine that cannibalism was not unknown. The state used the term 'the arduous march', a reference to Kim Il-sung's heroics in Manchuria. The command economy did slacken a little to allow small-scale market forces – touches of private enterprise – for the hard-pressed citizenry. It was difficult to ignore China's impressive economic growth based on market forces. North Korea also allowed some trade with South Korea – it was dubbed the 'sunshine policy'. As a result of the thaw, Kaesong industrial park was built in 2003 just north of the DMZ. But the economy remained stuck 'between the Victorian era and the worst days of Stalin'. Meanwhile the leader's cult status was layered with more and more unlikely accolades. He was supposed to possess supernatural powers such as never needing to go to the lavatory. The most famous story was the claim that he hit eleven holes in one the first time he played golf.

From 1994 North Korea started talking to the Americans about freezing the nuclear programme in exchange for aid. In 2000 Pyongyang agreed to a missile construction freeze. In 2002 the North Koreans admitted secret nuclear weapons production. That was the year the country joined America's hate list – the axis of evil. In 2003 the regime began six-party talks with China, Japan, Russia, South Korea and the USA about removing the nuclear weapons programme. Western intelligence agencies were abuzz with rumours that military hardliners opposed Kim's nuclear disarmament. On 9 October 2006 the North Korean government announced that it had successfully completed an underground nuclear test. The leader's cult continued unabated. Pyongyang claimed hero worship, while the outside world argued it was fear of the regime. US and South Korean sources said that in 2004 the state held 200,000 political prisoners in their gulags.

The Dear Leader was increasingly reclusive, partly – it was claimed – because of his poor health. During his seventeen-year reign he was recorded as having spoken just one single sentence in public. For years before 2008 it was rumoured that he had actually died and that one of his many doubles was standing in for him. Inevitably, the succession question kept coming up. Kim the Second's oldest son, Kim Jong-nam, was thought to be a possible next-generation heir. But he had been arrested at Tokyo's international airport in 2001 where he was attempting to enter Japan on a fake passport with the apparent intention of visiting Tokyo Disneyland. Intelligence chatter was that the Japanese had been tipped off by rivals in the regime. Kim Jong-nam was the son of an un-recognized and initially secret marriage between his father and the actress Song Hye-rim.

Movie buff

The Dear Leader was reputed to be a big fan of Elvis Presley. It was said that the bouffant hair, Vegas-era sunglasses and jumpsuits were influenced by the King of Rock 'n' Roll. Like Elvis, Kim loved pretty young girls. He was said by his detractors to love the Korean people but especially young virgins. Kim the Second also had an obsession with show business, especially films, throughout his life. Sean Connery and Elizabeth Taylor were said to be his favourite Western actors. In 1978, on Kim Jong-il's orders, Shin Sang-ok, a well-known South Korean film director, and his former wife, Choi Eun-hee, a beautiful actress, were kidnapped in order to revive the North Korean film industry.

Kim had joined the Propaganda and Agitation Department in 1966 and soon became director of the Motion Picture and Arts Division. He now had a library of over 15,000 films, some made in the West. Initially he produced his own films and operas with one main theme – the heroics of his father's fight against the Japanese. But he knew enough about foreign film production to realize that North Korean efforts were rather lifeless and one-dimensional. He wanted fresh blood for his pet projects. The South Korean star, Choi Eun-hee, was lured to Hong Kong on the pretext of directing a film. She was drugged and abducted in January 1978. She was housed in a luxury villa called Building Number One in the capital. Kim Jong-il took her to movies and operas and parties where he often chatted about films and asked Choi for her opinions. It was five years before she knew that she had been kidnapped as bait for her ex-husband, Shin Sang-ok. The film producer had fallen on hard times and was looking for movie opportunities. He had divorced Choi, and had a new family, but he went to Hong Kong to look for her. North Korean operatives had been waiting for him. He was also taken and also given lavish accommodation but not told about Choi. He kept trying to escape and was eventually imprisoned for three years but not brutalized. In February 1983 he was released and in March Shin and Choi were re-united at a party hosted by the Dear Leader.

They were asked to work for the regime, firstly by critiquing up to four films every day, mainly from the communist bloc. Kim Jong-il admitted that he wanted Shin to direct a film and enter it in an international contest. Kim understood that the DPRK's movie-making had to change in style and content. The kidnapped duo did make films and one did win an award at a Czechoslovak festival. The most elaborate and costly movie they produced was *Pulgasari*, a lurid Godzilla rip-off set in medieval Korea. Kim Jong-il was involved closely in the films produced by the couple; sometimes they were written by the Dear Leader himself. The couple did try to innovate, by using Eastern European actors for the first time and, very daringly, they showed a half-veiled kissing scene. The couple ingratiated themselves with Kim and they were allowed to travel to Czechoslovakia and Yugoslavia on film business but always surrounded by heavy-duty minders. Kim asked the couple to travel to Vienna to look for international finance for a film on Genghis Khan to be directed by the Dear Leader. In March 1986 they managed to slip their minders, around midnight, and literally run to the forewarned US embassy in the Austrian capital.

Shin later lived in the US and worked in the film industry before eventually moving back to South Korea. North Korea claimed that the couple had defected and had not been kidnapped. A book and a film documentary about their experiences were produced in 2015 and 2016 respectively. BBC's Radio Four also broadcast a dramatization of their saga in 2017.

Kim Jong-il's psychology

Intelligence experts in both Washington and Seoul spent much time on assessing the personality of Kim Jong-il. It was assumed that he shared many of the personality traits of fellow axis of evil leaders such as Saddam Hussein: that he was paranoid, sadistic, anti-social and narcissistic. The North Korean supremo prided himself on the country's alleged self-sufficiency despite the massive suffering of his often starving population. Like Saddam he was alleged to have palaces all over the country. Like Saddam, he feared assassination. And like his father, Kim Il-sung, he had a fear of flying, usually travelling in his personal armoured train, for example, for talks in China and Russia.

It was reported that he died on his train on 17 December 2011. In the end, in June 2009, it had been announced that Kim Jong-un, the youngest son, was anointed as the next leader. His official title was 'The Brilliant Comrade' and 'The Great Successor'.

Kim Jong-un

Kim 3 was certainly unique. The second hereditary leader in the same family in a supposedly communist nation was also one of the youngest heads of state in the world. It is true, however, that Fidel Castrol handed over to his brother in a communist polity. Yet North Korea has, so far, lasted longer than Cuban communism or their mutual mentor, the Soviet Union. Never a bleeding-heart liberal, the North Korean dictator ordered the execution of his uncle, Jang Song-thaek, and the assassination with VX poison of his half-brother, Kim Jong-nam. And yet despite his aggressive military policy Kim Jong-un met the South Korean leader, Moon Jae-in, twice; and then met the world's most powerful man, President Donald Trump, three times. The TV pictures of Kim's summits with President Putin and the Chinese leadership are broadcast endlessly in North Korea to prove that the young dictator is treated as an equal by world leaders.

Kim Jong-un was born on 8 January 1982 (according to North Korean sources) but the actual date was a year later. He was the second of three children born to Kim Jong-il. The older brother was considered effeminate and interested only in guitar music. His obsession with rock star Eric Clapton and lack of any political acumen meant that he would pose no threat and so could spend the rest of his life in a gilded cage. The third child, Kim Yo-jong, was born in 1987 and she came to be the dictator's closest personal assistant. Kim Jong-un's father had not married his mother, so technically the son was illegitimate according to North Korea's puritanical norms. His mother, Ko Yong-hui, had been born in Japan, a very black mark, and, even worse, her sister had defected. Despite this, Kim Jong-un was considered to be blessed with the cultural purity of the Paektu bloodline. This was like 'tracing your ancestors to the *Mayflower* but in totalitarian overdrive', in the graphic words of the dictator's biographer, Anna Fifield.

All three children of Kim Jong-il were reportedly educated in Switzerland. This later led to hopes for reform just as the young Bashar al-Assad of Syria had been partly educated in London and then had married an English-born and cultured and Westernized Syrian woman. And Mohammad bin Salman, the Crown Prince of Saudi Arabia, had enthusiastically toured Silicon Valley, and even allowed women to drive in his benighted country. Neither turned out to be reformers, despite the Western connections and all the hopes of Western observers. By all accounts, both at home and in Switzerland, the young Kim Jong-un led a spoiled and solitary upbringing. According to his very few Swiss schoolmates, he liked video games but was obsessed by basketball – which explained his later involvement with the highly eccentric former Chicago Bull, Dennis Rodman. The young Kim's mother was considered something of a tiger mother, despite her later absences. Yet even her devoted administrations could not fully explain the official North Korean hagiographies that boast Kim Jong-un firing a gun (accurately) at three and driving a truck at 80 miles an hour when he was just eight. He was not a bright student but he was later heralded as a 'genius among geniuses'. Kim Jong-un came home to study at Kim Il-sung university and then at its military equivalent. Whatever his military skills, he was later referred to as 'Comrade Marshal'. This elevated the new leader above all other military ranks.

When Kim was growing up he had a Japanese chef, Kenji Fujimoto, as a personal cook and as a surrogate playmate. Fujimoto remained fond of his young charge when he was allowed to return home. In later interviews, the Japanese talked of the chain-smoking leader's favourite brand being Saint Laurent cigarettes and that he was a heavy drinker, especially of Johnnie Walker whisky. That was the least of it – when he came to power, Kim 3 collected palaces and planes as well as luxury cars and boats. His father, Kim Jong-il, was eating caviar and lobster while his subjects were starving. During the height of the famine, he was importing almost a million dollars' worth of booze, especially Hennessy Paradis cognac. The Great Successor inherited the lavish taste in cuisine but did not seem to collect women in the way his playboy father did. To the contrary, Kim 3 started to parade his glamorous wife, Ri Sol-ju, in public, unprecedented in North Korean political life. They even attended the local version of rock concerts. This was all very modern and yet he dressed in a fashion only worn in communist holdout states. He wore the almost cartoonish hairstyle prompting Western jokes along the lines of 'If I were given a haircut like that, I would go nuclear too'. It was rumoured that he'd had plastic surgery to ape his grandfather; certainly he developed the low gravelly voice of Kim Il-sung. The old-fashioned clothes were supposed to remind North Koreans of the 'good old days' under the founder. Unlike his father, Kim 3 enjoyed public speaking even on televised presentations. Kim 2 was just five foot three inches tall, hence the Cuban heels. Kim 3 was just over five feet seven inches so maybe all the stretching playing basketball – a common Korean belief – may have helped the short man. When he came to power he did not exercise much if the expansion of his girth was anything to go by. Western and South Korean experts attributed his health problems – even though he was in his early thirties – to gout, hypertension and possible diabetes. The Kim royal family went to extraordinary lengths to avoid any intelligence agency collecting any evidence of Kim 3's health issues. The leader travelled with his own loo, for example, in case someone tried to analyze his regal stools. And all utensils and surfaces were scrupulously cleansed when he stayed abroad. At the same time, the extreme fastidiousness also included elaborate systems of food-tasters. Kim 3 did not want what happened to his half-brother to be visited on him.

The first two years are often the most dangerous in a transition in a dictatorship. Most outside observers expected the whole regime to tear itself apart under the young apprentice dictator. He appeared mad *and* bad, as well as inexperienced. Bad he may have been: the former defence minister was reduced to bits by anti-aircraft fire and his uncle, who had nurtured the transition, was secretly jailed, then publicly humiliated and finally shot, probably by a firing squad. But Kim 3 was not mad – everything was calculated to maintain his hold on power. He took control of both the party and the army perhaps more firmly than his father.

The military-first credo remained but the political role of the military was taken down a notch. Via high-level purges the position of the Korean Workers' Party was elevated relative to the armed forces. In the most surprising of his purges and political shake-ups, Kim Jong-un convened an unusual Sunday meeting of the party's central committee politburo on 16 July 2012 in order to remove the head of the army, Vice Marshal Ri Yong-ho. He had been one of four military officers among the seven casket-bearers at Kim Jong-il's funeral. Vice Marshal Ri had been considered to be a key mentor for the young new leader. In the following November, Kim Jong-gak, another pall bearer, and also a vice marshal, was purged. A third pall-bearer, U Tong-chuk, the boss of the secret police and spy agency, was also purged. These and other purged senior military officers symbolized a re-balancing of the party that had been increasingly subordinated during Kim Jong-il's reign. And this was one of the many reasons why Western intelligence experts looked to a possible military coup as the most likely means of possible reform via a military intervention. That scenario must have occurred to the Great Successor as well. The new young boss was also reported to have removed the military control over the regime's foreign currency operations, such as mineral exports and illegal dealings in arms and fake currency, a major source of prestige and income among the armed forces' elite. The role of the military in various party organs was downsized. The revitalized civilian approach was epitomized by the return of Pak Pong-ju, a prime minister from 2003–2007. In DPRK terms, he was considered something of an economic reformer.

And yet politics in the elite circles was never that simple – merely a slight re-assertion of party control over a spoiled military. True, 44 per cent of the top 218 military officers had been removed by Kim Jong-un. This did not mean a big shake-up in the elite, however. Just as in the pre-Japanese feudal system, the leadership's top families had intermarried. Since the 1950s the leadership had consisted of Kim Il-sung, his family and his guerrilla commanders. Because this elite had intermarried and was in its third generation, politics tended to be rows between families and their patronage networks. Powerful families inevitably had relatives ranged across the party and the military. So sometimes family disputes were configured as domestic policy issues or even international crises (such as nuclear weapons).

The 'military first' policy had always been dominant but Kim Jong-un understood that the economy had to improve as well. His people could have guns *and* butter – nukes and some loosening of state control of the economy. 'Reform' was never to be mentioned because that implied there was something wrong with an ideologically perfect system. Kim's uncle had been shot partly because his closeness to China had influenced him to dare to suggest that the next-door economic superpower could offer some possible examples. Smuggling and ubiquitous local markets organized with the use of mobile phones helped to tweak the socialist system a little, without taking a capitalist highway as in next-door China. Pyongyang underwent a construction boom – and the new buildings were not just party monoliths. Kim 3 allowed amusement parks, skating rinks and even a ski resort (near Wonsan). The altered skyline of the capital prompted some local wags to dub the new area 'Pyonghatten'. New apartments with two or three bedrooms went for up to $80,000 – when the average national monthly salary was still around $4. Just as in Russia, North Korea had grown a system of oligarchs – provided they toed the party's political line.

The nukes were still there. At the time of his accession, South Korean experts estimated that the DPRK's strategic weapons had cost around $3 billion over the previous fifteen years and the most recent missile launch had cost about $850 million, enough to buy 2.5 million tonnes of corn. And the costs did not include the loss of foreign trade and investment.

And yet Kim Jong-il did introduce a new style of leadership. He attended pop concerts performed by the Moranbong Band, a new all-girl musical group who had reportedly been selected by the leader himself. They donned short black dresses instead of the voluminous traditional clothing. They were better than the UK's Spice Girls in Britain in that they could actually sing and dance; and despite North Korea's reputation for famines, the Moranbong ladies looked far better fed than their British counterparts. Their lyrics were pure propaganda, admittedly, but tuneful propaganda. The new boss did lots of TV and media and went out pressing the flesh, especially during his many visits to army units. Meanwhile, the new media-savvy supremo clamped down on border security; defecting and smuggling halved. Instead, more North Koreans were encouraged – or forced – to go abroad as workers to earn currency for the government. Tens of thousands went to work in Russia, China and elsewhere. The regime pocketed about 75 per cent of their salaries although that still allowed the North Korean workers to earn five times more than they would have at home.

Kim Jong-un had always loved basketball – that probably explained his odd-couple friendship with the six-foot-seven-inch-tall former Chicago Bull sportsman, Dennis Rodman. He also played for the Detroit Pistons, the LA Lakers and the Dallas Mavericks. Originally very shy, Rodman became a consummate showman: he wore a wedding dress to promote his 1996 autobiography, for example. Heavily tattooed and pierced, he was famous for his female companions, most notably Madonna. Rodman was a well-known wrestler as well. The heavy-drinking exhibitionist also enjoyed reality TV stardom (and his own TV show), and this is how he met another famous showman, Donald Trump. So Rodman was the only man who could claim friendship with both eccentric leaders. The irreverent black B-lister sent the State Department foreign policy experts, with all their language skills and Ivy League degrees, into a state of real rage or sheer bemusement. Kim and Rodman talked basketball a lot and drank a lot. On one famous public occasion, Rodman gave a long rambling toast that ended with: 'Marshal, your father and grandfather did some fucked-up shit. But you, you're trying to change and I love you for that.'

Everyone held their breath. Eventually, Kim Jong-un smiled and raised his glass. Every North Korean present then exhaled.

Part of the reason for the new style was doing a deal with the Americans. Hence the weird utility of the badass Rodman. And it was also targeted at South Korea. Kim was not the only new leader on the peninsula. Park Geun-hye, of the conservative New Frontier Party, became the first female leader for thirteen centuries when she won a presidential election on 20 December 2012. And, like her northern counterpart, she was a child of the political elite. She had been born into Korean political royalty: her father, Park Chung-hee, led South Korea from 1963 until his assassination in 1979. She had previously filled in as first lady after her mother was killed in 1974 by a North Korean assassin who was aiming at her father. Park Geun-hye had campaigned on a policy of 'trustpolitik' – trade and humanitarian aid would be decoupled from the nuclear issue. Just before her inauguration the DPRK's third nuclear test temporarily scuppered her trustpolitik aspirations. North Korean propaganda cited 'the venomous swish of skirt' as a cause for renewed tensions on the peninsula. Despite his apparent reformist and modernizing tendencies, Kim Jong-un closed the Kaesong Industrial Complex, putting over 50,000 North Koreans out of work.

Despite such economic idiocies, a minority of North Koreans prospered to a large extent, while the vast majority saw some minor improvements especially in their diets. You could always tell when a North Korean had spent a little time in China – the grey pallor often associated with a very poor diet would disappear and the newcomer's skin would become more healthy and rosier. Nevertheless, under Kim 3, human rights abuses on a massive scale continued. A UN report recommended indicting the dictator at the International Criminal Court for crimes against humanity. But the deaths of thousands of North Koreans – because they were hidden – raised little publicity compared with the death of one American. Otto Frederick Warmbier was returned to the USA in a coma after being imprisoned in North Korea in 2016 for allegedly removing a poster of the Great Leader during a student visit. President Trump condemned the 'brutal' regime and described Kim as a 'madman' in June 2017. A little later when the President was cosying up to Kim, Trump said he believed the North Korean leader when he said he was not responsible for Warmbier's death.

Kim Jong-un rapidly secured his position by ruthless executions and total control of the state apparatus. He proved to the world that he had the nuclear weapons and the missiles to reach America (whether he could miniaturize the bombs to go on, and stay on, the missile tips was another matter). Kim would not be another Gaddafi. Nor would he suffer internal revolt because he could keep both his political and military/ security oligarchies under control while alleviating some of the economic hardships for the masses. Thus, secure at last, he ventured onto the world stage, to re-insure his flanks – Russia and China. Pyongyang had to talk to Seoul as well. And then Kim needed to deal with his prime adversary, the USA. Both alpha males, Kim Jong-un and Donald Trump, prided themselves on their personal diplomacy.

Koreans often described themselves as shrimps living among whales because of the big powers around their small country. Now the diminutive Great Successor was walking tall among the international players in China, Russia and above all the USA.

Chapter 5

Nukes

By 2019 North Korea had perhaps twenty to thirty nuclear weapons and also a sufficient stockpile of fissile material to produce a lot more. And they had done this largely on their own, admittedly while many North Koreans had starved to death. President Putin had once said that the North Koreans would rather 'eat grass' than give up their nuclear weapons. This proved to be literally true – during the famine years many North Koreans did eat various types of grass. Pyongyang also had large stores of chemical and biological munitions. Not surprisingly, the DPRK withdrew from the Non-Proliferation Treaty in 2003 and after 2006 it conducted a series of tests with bigger and bigger yields. Despite sanctions of increasing severity, North Korea continued to develop and test its modern arsenal, especially missile technology.

Ever since North Korea was threatened with the American use of nukes during the Korean War (1950–53), the regime had sought to defend itself by a self-sufficient nuclear deterrence. In 1962, when the USSR appeared to capitulate to the USA over their missiles in Cuba, Kim Il-sung had reckoned that Moscow was selling out its small ally for its own interests. Thus Pyongyang could not entrust its fundamental security to another power – the same kind of conclusion reached by President Charles de Gaulle. And once Richard Nixon had secured his rapprochement with Beijing, the ever-paranoid Kim Il-sung feared another possible sell-out. Privately, Kim Il-sung decided that his family stability depended on nukes. And probably he made the personal calculation that in lieu of charisma, his son, Kim Jong-il, could at least wave his nukes around.

Initially the USSR refused to help with military nuclear technology but agreed to assist with a civilian energy programme. Moscow helped to train North Korean scientists. Later, Beijing refused to support Pyongyang's nuclear ambitions. Soviet engineers meanwhile assisted with the construction of the Yongbyon Nuclear Scientific Research

Centre and supervised the construction of the first reactors. The weapons project began in the early 1980s; the state initially ratified the Non-Proliferation Treaty yet dragged its feet regarding demands from the International Atomic Energy Authority (IAEA), especially regarding on-site inspection, until 1992. In the following year the inspection question caused North Korea to withdraw. As the IAEA strongly suspected, the regime had a lot to hide.

Then Washington decided to get involved. In 1994, under the Agreed Framework, the USA said it would supply two light-water reactors for civilian energy provided Pyongyang agreed to give up its weapons programme. Republican opposition in Congress during the Clinton presidency led to the breakdown of the agreement. By 2002 the US policy of providing aid for a civilian programme was abandoned. Instead, North Korea bribed the Pakistani nuclear establishment for technology just as Saudi Arabia paid Islamabad for access to nukes in case Iran got them. Dr A.Q. Khan, the rogue inventor of Pakistan's nuclear bomb, allegedly sold the technology secrets to both North Korea and Iran.

Pyongyang surprised the Americans by admitting in late 2002 that it had been secretly building weapons despite the 1994 agreement with Washington. Was this just a rash piece of rogue diplomacy or a calculated tactical move by a shrewd dictator who wanted to exploit America's pre-occupation with the build-up to the war in Iraq, and thus squeeze out some more concessions? Under Bill Clinton, the policy had been to work with North Korea but even the Democratic president had serious plans to attack the burgeoning nuclear programme. When George W. Bush took over, the policy was much tougher – the president called Kim Jong-il a 'pygmy' and said he 'loathed' him. North Korea formally left the NPT that it had anyway treated as a diplomatic joke.

On 9 October 2006 North Korea announced that it had conducted its first underground nuclear test. Pyongyang had informed Beijing only twenty minutes beforehand. China was told that the yield would be 4 kilotons; foreign seismic readings, however, put the yield at 0.5 to 0.9 kiloton. Even the advertised yield was small in comparison with the first tests of other countries: Pakistan's first test, for example, in 1998, was about 9 kilotons. The first French test in 1960 yielded 60 kilotons but France had an advanced economy and no sanctions. Experts conjectured that North Korea's small yield may have been deliberate as part of its miniaturization process. Or the DPRK was conserving its small plutonium stockpile and possibly minimizing radioactive emissions. Some in the Western intelligence community questioned whether a proper nuclear test had been conducted at all. Other US sources confirmed that the air samples showed the test device to have been made from plutonium and not enriched uranium.

In a technical sense the test was 'a fizzle'. Nevertheless North Korea could now declare that it was a nuclear-weapon state. Whether the device was usable and reliable as a deliverable weapon was another question. Politically, the fizzle mattered a lot, however. In every way the south had outdone the DPRK. Now the northern state could boast that it had outperformed its southern kin in a key area: advanced technology. Moreover, the test came on the same day that the UN Security Council approved the South Korean foreign minister, Ban Ki Moon, as the next UN secretary general. At least the DPRK was in the lead in one important sector, even while it was still a political outcast.

Within a few months the regime officially confirmed that it had acquired nuclear weapons. Was this finally a sufficient deterrent against the American superpower that the paranoid regime so feared?

Pyongyang was a world-class player in on-off diplomacy: of 'cheat and retreat'. It offered to shut down its main nuclear facility during the so-called six-party talks. The members were the two Koreas, China, Russia, Japan and the USA. Dismantling its main facility would be in exchange for aid and a normalization of relations with Japan and USA.

The main 5MW(e) reactor, on the plains at Yongbyon, was surrounded by mountains. Located in Yongbyon County in North Pyongan Province, about 100 kilometres north of Pyongyang, by 2007 it was producing around 6kg of plutonium a year, roughly enough for one or, just possibly, two weapons. The DPRK had only enough fuel then for a partial reloading of the reactor and its fuel-fabrication plant had deteriorated while it was shut done down under the Agreed Framework. A new 50MW (e) reactor – if completed – would have increased by tenfold North Korea's production of plutonium but it remained in bad repair because of the difficulties in importing equipment and materials.

By 2007 it was estimated in the West that the DPRK had enough separated plutonium for between five to ten weapons, assuming that each contained between 4 to 5kg of plutonium. The DPRK's fleet of Russian Il-28 bombers was one possible means of delivery but the regime was busily producing smaller bombs that could be carried by the No-dong missile. The DPRK then had about 200 of the No-dong missiles as well as approximately 600 Scuds, according to American intelligence estimates.

For a while peace intruded on the DPRK's Armageddon option. Eventually the IAEA confirmed the closure of the Yongbyon reactor and North Korea began to receive some humanitarian aid. But this process collapsed in 2009 when North Korea launched a satellite that confirmed its advances in rocket technology. For good measure the regime then tested a bigger weapon in the north-eastern part of North Korea. This was relatively close to the Chinese border; the ensuing earthquake at the test site did not endear the regime to its northern protector.

The nuclear tests managed to unify even the UN Security Council. On 12 June 2009, in a unanimous vote, Resolution 1874 was passed. It authorized UN members to seize any North Korean cargo on land, sea or air that was connected with the nuclear programme. It was not very effective because both China and South Korea were very reluctant to use force to support the embargo. The resolution mandated Pyongyang to return to the six-party talks and to re-join the Non-Proliferation Treaty. It instructed UN members to stop all loans and financial aid – except for humanitarian purposes – that could be diverted into the nuclear weapons' programme. It also tightened up the existing conventional arms embargo on the regime. Above all, it told North Korea to cease its nuclear weapons' ambitions.

In another swing of the diplomatic pendulum, in early 2012 North Korea announced that it would suspend uranium enrichment and stop testing while productive talks with Washington were again in play. The USA agreed to ship in humanitarian supplies and IAEA inspectors would be allowed in once more. Pyongyang, however, seemed unable to contain itself – in April 2012 the regime conducted a long-range missile test and soon began to say that its missiles could reach Alaska – as a 'gift for the American bastards'. Washington pulled out of the aid programme.

On 12 February 2013 the pariah state organized another underground test. North Korea said that it had succeeded in producing a big yield with a small bomb – the obvious step towards miniaturization for missile warheads. Western experts speculated that the yield was between 4 and 8 kilotons, larger than the first tests in 2006 and 2009. Although the DPRK claimed it had mastered miniaturization, it did not indicate whether the device was based on plutonium or highly enriched uranium; radioactive isotopes collected in Japan two months after the test had decayed too severely to determine a specific 'signature'. Many in the Western intelligence community believed that a uranium–based bomb had been detonated. If true, this indicated that North Korea had found a second path to nuclear weapons that was both easier to conceal than plutonium and much easier to sell because it could be more easily fashioned into a crude weapon, even for non-state actors such as al-Qaeda. North Korea continued to sell all sorts of arms including nuclear to all and sundry. Pyongyang had helped Syria build its nuclear plant until the Israelis bombed it in September 2007. And, in the Israeli view, North Korea acted as a 'duty free shop' for Iran, selling especially missiles for its proxies, notably Hezbollah and Hamas.

On 8 May 2015 North Korea announced that it had completed its first test of an SLBM (submarine-launched ballistic missile). The local media glorified in the country's 'Sputnik moment'. The pictures appeared to show a missile modelled on the Soviet R-27 Zyb missile that had a range of 2,400 kilometres.

In January 2016 Pyongyang claimed it had tested a hydrogen bomb although most Western experts disputed the claim to have crossed over the thermonuclear threshold. A month after the alleged hydrogen test, North Korea claimed to have launched a satellite into orbit while insisting that it was purely for peaceful scientific purposes. Many military specialists assumed that it was an ICBM test – which spooked the Chinese as well as Washington.

Nevertheless, the stubborn regime conducted its fifth nuclear test in September 2016. In March that year the UN Security Council voted to impose additional sanctions on North Korea. Undaunted, North Korea pushed ahead. But the climax of the nuclear braggadocio was the arrival of the Pink Lady on DRPK TV screens. Ri Chun-hee was a veteran newscaster who is usually brought out to announce major occasions. She is known as the Pink Lady because she wears a cerise robe. The nation shivers if she is frowning but on 3 September 2017 she was smiling broadly. She announced 'the completion' of the state's nuclear programme because a successful test of a hydrogen bomb had been achieved. Literally, shock waves went around the world. The needles showed that around 100,000 tons of TNT had exploded, roughly five times the size of the 'Fat Man' bomb that wiped out Nagasaki. The accession to the thermonuclear club made the PDRK a much more dangerous beast on the world stage. The North Korean media showed beaming photographs of the 77-year-old Ri Hong-sop, the country's top nuclear scientist, standing alongside a delighted Kim Jong-un.

In 2017 two further ICBMs were launched. Now Kim Jong-un could reach continental USA – not just the outlier of Guam or, then, Alaska. Whether the warheads were sufficiently small and heat-resistant to go on top of these ICBMs was another matter. But the country's scientific progress had been remarkable for such a small, impoverished and isolated state. The DPRK had some foreign help, true, but mostly through trial and error, endless determination and skill plus lots of money, they had joined a very exclusive H-bomb club.

Yet North Korea was driving itself into extreme isolation by, for example, launching four missiles into the Sea of Japan in March 2017. In the previous month Beijing, incensed by the behaviour of its unruly protégé, announced it was suspending all imports of coal from North Korea as part of UN sanctions. China often honoured such measures in their breach rather than their fulfilment but this time the screws were tightened a little bit more than was needed for public relations' purposes.

On 15 April 2017 North Korea staged a massive military parade to mark the 105th anniversary of the birth of the founder, Kim Il-sung. The parade included two land-based ICBM canisters as well as a submarine-launched version of the same type. Whether the contents of the canisters worked was another matter. And in the past much of the missile technology on show bore the hallmarks of manufacture in the People's Republic of China. The original missiles were derived from Soviet Scuds but they grew more sophisticated with Chinese help and soon took on the appearance of Chinese ICBMs, both land- and submarine-based.

North Korea continued its role as a prolific arms exporter as well as importer. The Korea Mining and Development Trading Corporation (KOMID) sold conventional weapons around the world. It sold missile technology to Iran and gunboats and artillery systems throughout Africa, South America and the Middle East. It sold to both states and terrorist movements; for example North Korea was a key supplier for the Tamil Tigers during their long insurgency in Sri Lanka.[1] One of Pyongyang's closest secret relationships was with the ever nuclear-incontinent Pakistan. North Korea had a front company, Hap Heng, based in Macau, which dealt in missile technology with Islamabad. Pakistan's medium-range missile, the Ghauri, was suspiciously similar to North Korea's Rodong 1. Pyongyang was also reported to have supplied missile technology to Syria and Yemen and also armed Libya when Colonel Gaddafi was in power.

In July 2017 North Korea launched a Hwasong-14 missile. It flew 930 kilometres and landed in the waters of Japan's exclusive economic zone. Some of the earlier tests had resulted in embarrassing misfires but this time Washington estimated that the flight trajectory and duration (39 minutes) meant that the missile could have reached all of Alaska. Then Pyongyang fired another ICBM and Western scientists reckoned that this could have landed in the continental USA. Whether the missiles were accurate or not, it was clear to American defence planners that North Korea was close to being able to launch a nuclear-tipped ICBM against the American mainland and, with no difficulty, hit targets in Japan or, of course, South Korea. After over eighty missile tests between 2013 and 2017, Kim Jong-un could boast publicly that he had 'finally realized the great historic cause of completing the state nuclear force'. Now the Great Successor could be strong enough to deal with the bullying American superpower. The regime also had one of the largest arsenals of chemical and biological weapons. It was alleged that the stockpiles of up to 5,000 metric tons of chemical weapons ranked North Korea third after the USA and Russia. Pyongyang was also in the forefront of cyber warfare.

Despite all the aggressive rhetoric by Pyongyang, it was highly unlikely that North Korea would ever start a nuclear war. The far more powerful USA would destroy the country in a counter-strike, no matter how few, if any, North Korean missiles actually reached, and exploded, in America. Nuclear weapons were a means of regime survival and, more important,

Kim family survival. Most of the regime's rhetoric was about defensive deterrence although occasionally statements were issued that hinted that nukes might be used pre-emptively if the USA was about to attack. North Korea probably had the H-bomb and the missiles to reach the American heartland. It made no sense to actually use them, however. The danger of accidental warfare amid such heavily charged rhetoric on such a heavily armed peninsula was obvious. War by accident, not design, haunted the world.

Washington wanted the one thing Pyongyang could not give up – its nuclear deterrence. One way or another North Korea had reneged on every nuclear deal it made. Was North Korea the same as Iran – Washington could not live with Iranian nukes? But North Korea had long possessed what they called their 'treasured sword'. Could the USA ever make a deal with a dynastic regime that held on to just few 'bombs in the basement' – the policy originally pursued by Washington's allies, the Israelis?

Many American negotiators grew weary of North Korea's endless broken promises. As Robert Gates, the US Defense Secretary, said in 2010: America 'was tired of buying in the same horse twice'. His boss, President Barack Obama, preferred to use the more diplomatic phrase, 'strategic patience'.

Chapter 6

Inside the Beast

The structure of the system

The Democratic People's Republic of Korea describes itself as a self-reliant socialist state and, stressing its 'democracy', formally holds regular elections. The elections so far have been a total sham in the neo-Stalinist dictatorship. It is probably more authoritarian than even Stalinism because of the Orwellian ubiquity of control that was not available in Joseph Stalin's day. And the Kim dynasty has forged a personality cult far more intrusive than Stalin's or Mao's. Kim Jong-il developed a concept of 'The Admitted', a tiny circle of the elite whose presence the dictator had personally requested and who had spent more than twenty minutes with him behind closed doors. This was rather like the British Privy Council twinned with a senior Ku Klux Klan meeting.

Juche – self-reliance – was introduced into the constitution in 1972. The means of production are owned by the government through state-run enterprises and agriculture; since Kim Jong-un came to power, however, some minor free enterprise has been allowed, not least the ubiquitous local markets. They were dubbed 'frog markets' because they were initially closed down by the police but then they jumped up elsewhere. Services such as education, healthcare and largescale food production are heavily subsidized or state run. This is called the Public Distribution System (PDS) that determines the nationwide allocation of necessities, especially food coupons. During the early 1990s the state system, especially for food production and distribution, broke down, leading to famine on a vast scale. (It was later re-introduced by Kim Jong-un.) The International Monetary Fund said in 1998 that industrial production had declined by at least 60 per cent in the previous five years. Workers cannibalized parts of the moribund machinery in factories and industrial sites to sell as scrap to buy food. Real human cannibalism was rumoured as well. In 1999 reports emerged of dirt-poor Koreans selling their young daughters to Chinese farmers as brides, because they could no longer feed their families. Millions starved to death but often foreign NGOs could not help. In 1998, for example, Médecins Sans Frontières left because of excessive controls on their work. A British Red Cross doctor who worked for one year in North Korea at the end of the great famine noted that even supposedly privileged soldiers and junior party workers were 'cachectic' (extremely emaciated); the doctor also said that, because of shortages of conventional medicines in the hospitals, the ordinary citizens relied on traditional Korean natural remedies. The one thing that impressed the doctor, however, was the very smart-looking traffic policewomen directing the almost non-existent traffic.[1] By the end of the 1990s the worst of the hunger years were over, although the authoritative International Institute for Strategic Studies in London said that 'This may not be famine but it is slow starvation.' Soon the male gerontocrats who ran the administration decided to eject nearly all NGOs.

The policy of spending first on the military and nuclear programme *(Songun)* completely skewed the economy and contributed to the food shortages and general breakdown in infrastructure and services. North Korea had the highest percentage of any world population involved in security (military/para-military/police): 37 per cent. It also has the fourth (arguably) largest standing army on the planet; the active army stands at just over 1.2 million with numerous reserve systems and militias that add up to 9.5 million trained citizens. (For details of the military see Appendix 1.)

The politics have been utterly rigid, although the famine years frayed some restrictions as many people stopped their often non-existent work to forage for food in the countryside or operate in black-market work. Sometimes even disciplined soldiers robbed peasants and shopkeepers for food, at gunpoint. Despite the numerous hardships, the DPRK's most recent constitution (2016) still emphasized the *Juche* and *Songun* concepts, plus the 'Ten Principles of the One-Ideology System'. This was supposed to be a guide for all North Koreans. The Korean Workers' Party (KWP) boasted three million members (out of a population of an estimated 25 million). Technically, the KWP operated as a multi-party front (The Democratic Front for the Reunification of the Fatherland) but the satellite organizations have had little or no influence. The three Kims, dead or alive, controlled everything. Kim Jong-un is the chairman of the party and supreme commander of the army, though his dead grandfather became the 'Eternal President'. Even the embalmed Lenin was never given such an active post-mortem role. The State Affairs Commission of North Korea was compared with a classic executive. The legislature is the unicameral Supreme People's Assembly; its 687 members are 'elected' every five years by universal suffrage. The members are hand-picked party officials and so the Assembly serves merely as a rubber stamp. There is also a cabinet which is headed by a prime minister. Despite all the polite names such as 'democratic' and 'people's' the fossilized political system can best be compared to an absolute monarchy or hereditary dictatorship.

Although socialism and democracy are misnomers, the basic ideology of *Juche* can genuinely be said to be ingrained in the Korean soul. Koreans regard themselves as one nation – all part of *Chosun*, the way North Koreans refer to their country. Koreans have always regarded themselves as a very hardy race, xenophobic, used to tough conditions, and natural warriors – because of their centuries-long struggle for independence. The conflicts with the neighbouring Russians, Chinese, Japanese and then Americans have inspired a genuine desire for a resilient form of independence, despite all the foreign aid. Notwithstanding the long Chinese cultural influence, the Koreans developed their own unique culture, a frozen sociology that has proved resilient. The Japanese occupation from 1910 to 1945 imposed a cultural assimilation where Koreans were forced to learn and speak Japanese, adopt Japanese names and the Shinto religion. The Korean language was banned in schools and public places. By the 1980s the ethnic nationalism of *Juche* had completely replaced the original polite subservience to Marxist-Leninism and later ideological nods towards Maoism. The philosophy of the DPRK's Spartan nationalism has been compared with the imperial *Showa* system in Japan or some former fascist movements in Europe.

Real power emanates from the Kim dynasty. The bloodline from the sacred Mount Paektu, where the cult myth says the dynasty was born, has to be maintained 'eternally' – nobody outside the family can therefore hope to aspire to the supreme leadership of the DPRK. This is not just genealogical determinism but also holistic politics where all art, music, literature, architecture and sculpture have to glorify the Kim dynasty. Though de facto the Kims have been made almost gods, they have been attributed with supernatural but not divine powers. The much-touted 'on-the-spot guidance' provided by the supreme leaders, where all the real experts around try to take down every precious word in little notebooks, suggests that the polymath Kim Jong-il was a master in whatever he encountered – especially military and economic matters. Statues and pictures of the leader can be found everywhere. Whether in state-controlled apartments or civic buildings, usually a special person is appointed to ensure that every day the mounted photograph of Kim Jong-un is immaculately clean. In the town and cities devoted followers, apparently spontaneously, sweep the steps up to the national political shrines. Kim Jong-un has hinted that he did not want to inherit the same hero-worship cult as his father whose birthday is one of the most important public holidays in the country. At such events children receive small presents in school – probably the only present the average child gets in the year. The idea is to emphasize the benevolent generosity of the great leader. A certain percentage of the population, the true believers or truly brainwashed, show genuine devotion to the demigods who rule them; the majority no doubt feel they have to be seen to pay homage. Any minor disrespect to the leadership could be noted by the omnipresent informer system, even within families, and the guilty can be led off to harsh re-education camps, or execution in some cases.

Security controls

The regime has shown some apparent flexibility – or manipulative diplomacy – in world affairs but its domestic internal control has changed little since the Cold War, though most citizens have cell phones but without access to international networks. Human Rights Watch has called North Koreans 'some of the world's most brutalized people' because of the regime's atrocious human rights record. The population is strictly micro-managed by the state; in all aspects – from jobs to dating and food supplies – the party dominates almost everything. This might imply an efficient totalitarian state but all North Koreans know how totally incompetent their system is, not least because it cannot even provide sufficient food. The utterly bureaucratic state comprises numerous fiefdoms where all the ministries are in constant tension and friction with each other. The administrative buildings, even in the capital, hardly ever have anything to denote what they do. Even civil servants in next-door and similar government offices usually do not know what the adjacent ministries are up to. And they very rarely talk to each other, let alone pay their comrades a visit, just as the political apparatchiki and the military tend to ignore each other at the lower levels.

What matters has always been total devotion to the party, state and leadership. Internal – let alone external – travel is carefully controlled by the Ministry of People's Security. That includes, for example, requiring permission to stay overnight with friends or family. That could be a crime against the code. Far worse would be a political offence. The State Security Department has imprisoned hundreds of thousands without due process. 'Hostiles' such as Christians or even someone who might have been overheard making a joke about food shortages – or, Heaven forbid, the magnificence of the Kims – have been dragged off to labour camps, without trial. Often their families used to be interned as well, sometimes for life; and frequently without knowing what offence they had committed. This was more than Orwellian, it was Kafkaesque. Amnesty International estimated recently that 200,000 prisoners were held in six immense concentration camps. Figures have varied, however; the US State Department estimated that up to 120,000 political prisoners were held in the main political prison camps.

Many inmates have been worked to death. Party members who have deviated have sometimes been deemed rehabilitated after extensive 're-education' and they have been given back their old jobs (but then carefully supervised). Satellite imagery and very extensive interviews with defectors have provided much information to Western NGOs. Very detailed evidence has been recorded of slave labour, endemic torture, starvation, organized rape, murder, forced abortions and even Nazi-style medical experimentation. Sexual violence in prisons and camps has been endemic. Guards and police have been able to abuse females almost at will and have never been prosecuted.

The North Korean state operates a legal system that is influenced by Japanese traditions and communist legal theory. The Supreme Court stands at the apex of the judicial structure with the 'people's courts' at the local levels; in addition there are military courts. Technically the legal system differentiates between civil and ordinary criminal matters and ideological crimes. Political prisoners are despatched to labour camps, while common-or-garden murderers and robbers are sent to a separate, slightly less harsh, penal system. The latter have a better chance of eventually getting out alive.

The Ministry of People's Security controls the national police force, investigates non-political crimes and runs the associated penal system. The State Security Department traditionally conducts domestic and foreign intelligence work and manages the camps for political prisoners. They can be shorter term for re-education or lifetime detention. This security apparatus has spies in nearly every accommodation block. The State Security Department also monitors phones and digital communications.

Society

Besides the very rigid social controls, North Korea was a very homogenous and disciplined society to start with. The minorities, ethnic Chinese and Japanese, are very small. The population in mid-2019 was estimated at 25.7 million, far smaller than could have been predicted, partly because famine blighted at least a generation. Domestic food production improved in the twenty-first century and food aid continued from international donors. But the World Food Programme reported a continuing lack of dietary diversity as well as poor access to proteins and fats. Besides famine, late marriage after lengthy conscription, shortage of housing, long work hours and lengthy political studies, for the party's true believers or simply the ambitious, exhaust the population. Very puritanical controls and strict family attitudes plus extended families in crowded dwellings also reduce the chances of dating. Even couples holding hands in public in North Korea is frowned upon. Every single defector or refugee who manages to reach South Korea always says that the one single thing that shocks them most is that people in South Korea kiss in public!

In the last decade or so far fewer people have died of outright starvation, although malnourishment continues. Yet the life expectancy of the average North Korean is around 70. Every individual possesses a lifetime health card containing a supposedly detailed medical record. A form of free national health service exists but the quality varies according to region and whether in town or countryside. Interviews with defectors all confirmed the lack of equipment and drugs and even anaesthetics for operations. According to the World Health Organization, spending per capita on health is one of the lowest anywhere. By choice, and necessity, many citizens rely on traditional remedies and preventive medicine via fitness and sport that are constantly encouraged by the regime.

The population has always been literate (although finding paper to write on has been very difficult – people used to write on the margins of newspapers). Education is compulsory for eleven years. The system encourages tertiary study, not least to provide scientists to produce rockets and fight cyber wars. There are an estimated 300 colleges and universities. The problem with tertiary education has been the lack of choice, not least the endless compulsory ideology classes; this can comprise up to 50 per cent of the curriculum, although more recently in the sciences this has been reduced. In schools, however, English and Russian were taught extensively.

All Koreans in both states speak the same language. As in all countries dialects and associated country bumpkin jokes abound. The northerners regard their version of Korean as more cultured and view the Seoul dialect as degenerate because of the adoption of Chinese and, especially, English words. Northerners, being more puritanical about their language purity (like the French), have tried to eliminate Chinese or European words; Chinese characters have also disappeared from the modern Hangul alphabet. Kim Jong-il apparently told the Russians that he could understand only 80 per cent of what his southern counterpart said. And yet, more recently, privileged children in Pyongyang have started aping the South Korean dialect and slang they hear from K-pop music and smuggled DVDs. There has been more openness to both southern dialect and even foreign languages in the north. It was once common in Pyongyang for locals to cross the road to avoid engaging with foreigners, not least to avoid problems with the security police.

Officially the DPRK has always been an atheist state, even though the mother of the state's founder served as a Presbyterian deaconess.

Technically, the constitution guarantees freedom of religion and the right to worship, although Amnesty International has criticized the regime for religious persecution. American missionaries have complained of extreme persecution, suggesting that Christians suffer more in the DPRK than anywhere else in the world. After once being a centre for Christianity perhaps fewer than 2 per cent practise that religion today. Korean shamanism, a kind of traditional animism, mixed with Buddhism and Taoism, is far more common. As is Chondoism, a cult developed in the early nineteenth century as a reaction to Western culture; it has been permitted but controlled by the state. Buddhism and Confucianism have a less formal but important implicit impact on cultural life, however.

Visual arts – especially along the lines of socialist realism – have been very popular propaganda tools. As in the old Soviet Union, membership of the Artists' Union was made compulsory. The Mansudae Art Studio was established in 1959 and became probably the biggest art factory in the world. It has made major statues especially for governments in Africa. The Heroes Acre in both Zimbabwe and Namibia display heroic guerrilla figures but the locals have been amused that their African legends all look Asiatic.

The state's messages are also conveyed by the so-called revolutionary operas based on traditional Korean themes. The *Sea of Blood* is the most performed in the PDRK as well as in China. The State Symphony Orchestra performs many of the Western classics as well. In February 2008 the New York Philharmonic Orchestra played in the capital and the concert was broadcast nationally. K-pop music – including the famous Gangnam style – has entered the country illegally and the government tried to compete with the all-girl Moranbong Band.

All the book publishing companies have been government owned. Mostly they churn out ideological educational materials as well as numerous volumes of Kim Il-sung. Some translations of foreign writers, including Shakespeare, have been printed in limited numbers. Under Kim Il-sung the epic novel was encouraged but under his son the trend shifted to shorter praise poems – cynics assumed that the paper shortages also helped to dictate the change in literary fashion. Under Kim Jong-il all citizens had to learn by heart three poems ('For my One and Only Homeland', 'Mother' and 'My Homeland'.)

Songbun

Formally *chulsin-songbun,* this is a traditional system that denotes status. It is a form of caste based on an individual's ancestors as well as behaviour over generations. *Songbun* relates to social and economic background but above all political loyalty to the regime. The system has given access to jobs, housing, party membership, education and food. Codified during the purges in the late 1950s, the party estimated that the population could be divided into friendly, neutral and hostile forces. In 1958 Kim Il-sung delineated the three classes: the loyal 'core class' (25 per cent); the 'wavering class' (55 per cent); and the 'hostile class' (20 per cent). *Songbun* has around fifty sub-classifications; it is akin to the Indian caste system mingled with South African apartheid. Unlike apartheid, however, in North Korea, through exceptional service, some mobility between the castes was possible. The regime always insists that all citizens are equal. And, under Kim Jong-un, a rich business oligarchy has emerged that has transcended *songbun,* provided they keep out of any hint of political opposition, on the Putin model. In short, money more than social background dictates status. Also, with the breakdown of society during the famine years the practice of punishing whole families for an individual's crimes declined. Nevertheless, defectors from the country still emphasize the impact of *songbun.*

The highest status traditionally denotes those, and later the families of those, who had fought alongside Kim Il-sung in the war against the Japanese. The system also nodded towards the classic definition of the proletariat and peasantry by privileging those at the start of the regime who were workers and peasants. Most of the top group became members of the Workers' Party. The middle group constituted the average citizen, while the hostile caste was defined as comprising subversive elements such as former landowners, those who had collaborated with the Japanese or perhaps Christians.

From the age of 17 every citizen has a file compiled by security and party officials. These are supposed to be updated every two years. It has been much easier to be downgraded, go down the snakes, rather than move up the ladder. Adultery with a workmate can secure black marks as can an off-hand remark about the party. If a relative commits a criminal or ideological offence, that can also work against an innocent relative. In the early days of the regime it had been possible to conceal a person's *songbun* especially if the citizen was leading an irreproachable and perhaps rural life. During Mao's cultural revolution and the resulting souring of relations with Beijing, Kim Il-sung feared Chinese intervention. And so the *songbun* system was tightened up and made more public. American Barbara Demick, in her excellent 2010 book on North Korean society, *Nothing to Envy*, described the caste system as 'combining Confucianism and Stalinism'. She said that a bad family background has been called 'tainted blood' and that it could last for three generations. She maintained that her extensive interviews with defectors indicated that some children grew up without knowing that they had bad *songbun*.[2] Other experts on North Korea have argued that the caste system was made more public, even while its importance declined.

Songbun – not least by dictating the supply of food coupons – could effectively exert centralized control over nearly every aspect of North Korean society. After the collapse of aid from the Soviet bloc, during the mid to late 1990s the allocation of jobs and food broke down almost completely. *Songbun* could then mean the difference between starvation and survival. Inevitably, some sort of free enterprise emerged not least in growing and selling food. Some of the lower caste, less dependent upon state benefits, started to engage in local food markets and smuggling, if they lived near the Chinese border. Their children were starving to death and black marks from the security police meant less, especially as the police were often starving themselves. Corruption became endemic. The catch phrase at police road blocks was 'Have you done your homework?' That was the code for requesting a bribe. Job promotion through military service became far less profitable – better to go into the booming private economy. *Muyok* (trade) became more lucrative than working for the party or army. Implicitly *songbun* remained important to the ruling party elite but most North Koreans chased money rather than ideological status.

One of the best-known examples of the decline of *songbun* revolved around Ko Yong-hui, the mother of the current leader, Kim Jong-un. She was born in Japan of Korean heritage. Technically this would put her in the hostile class, not least because her father had worked for the

Kim Il–sung in later life. The state was created and dominated by him.

US General Douglas MacArthur with the first president of South Korea, Syngman Rhee.

Mk 4 US 'Fat Man' atomic bomb. Not long after they were used in anger in Japan, some experts believed that they could be used again in the Korean War.

US General Mathew B. Ridgway, the man who took over after MacArthur was sacked. (*US Department of Defense*)

Lockheed P-80 Shooting Star, the first jet fighter used operationally by the USAF in Korea.

Korean War correspondent John Thomas Ward who worked for the *Baltimore Sun*.

Korea is often called 'the forgotten war' but there is a poignant war memorial in Washington. (*Author*)

Kim Jong-il took over from his father Kim Il-sung in 1994, the first example of a son inheriting a communist throne.

The Panmunjom meeting place in the DMZ. (*US DoD*)

The ubiquitous badge worn by North Koreans, whether or not they are party members.

The USS *Pueblo* was the first American ship captured without a fight since the nineteenth century. It was seized in January 1968. It is now a part of a war museum in the North Korean capital.

The ROKS *Cheoson* was sunk on 6 March 2010 by a North Korean torpedo. (*Republic of Korea, Ministry of Defence*)

Kim Jong-un succeeded his father in 2011.

The North Korean dictator had unusual 'friends', besides Donald Trump. A 2001 picture of Dennis Rodman, the former baseball star and celebrity wild man.

The capital of Pyongyang underwent something of a construction boom after Kim Jong-un came to power.

Despite little traffic, foreigners are always impressed by the immaculate female traffic police in Pyongyang.

The US THAAD system was installed in South Korea as a defence against the DPRK's missile threats. (*US DoD*)

A live-fire exercise of an MIA2 Abrams tank at the Rodriguez live-fire complex in South Korea in November 2017. (*US DoD, picture by Sgt Patrick Eakin*)

US and South Koreans during exercises in South Korea in April 2016. (*US DoD, Cpl Erick Loarca*)

Air Force Airman 1st Class Jocelyn Fonseca charges an M2 machine gun during a weapons' qualification training event at Camp Rodriguez, South Korea, May 2017. (*US DoD, photo by Gwendalyn Smith*)

A serviceman jumps from a US Navy MH-53E Sea Dragon helicopter during a mine-warfare training event for US and South Korean forces in Busan, October 2017. (*US DoD, Seaman William Carlisle*)

US Navy Seaman Eyob Adera performs a safety watch as an F/A-18E Super Hornet launches from the flight deck of the USS *Ronald Reagan* during INVINCIBLE SPIRIT, an exercise off the southern coast of South Korea, October 2016. (*US DoD, Nathan Burke*)

A USAF B-1B Lancer flying over the Korean peninsula prepares to receive fuel from a KC-135 Stratotanker from Andersen Air Force Base in Guam, August 2017. (*US DoD, Sgt Joshua Smoot*)

US Vice-President Mike Pence shakes hands with officers of the Combined Forces Command near the DMZ, April 2017. (*US DoD, Sgt K. Sharp*)

President Moon Jae-in of South Korea meets his northern counterpart in 2018 – part of the sunshine policy.

New best friends, Kim and Trump;
the two alpha males shake hands at the
Hanoi summit in February 2019.

South Koreans start dismantling some of the loudspeakers that pumped out propaganda over the DMZ. (*US DoD*)

Imperial Japanese Army. *Songbun* has traditionally passed via the father, not the mother, but it was easy to see why the current Great Leader is less keen on the old caste feudalism, quite apart from his desire to modernize the economy.

The economy

After the ravages of the Korean War, Chinese and Soviet aid helped to rebuild the DPRK's economy – for a while the north overtook the south in economic progress. After 1960 the weaknesses of the Soviet-style five-year plans began to become obvious. The shortage of arable land, the unreliable supply of energy, shortages of skilled labour as well as skewed socialist planning meant that the realities on the ground could not match the grandiose declarations of the state plans. One of the simple solutions was for the regime to stop issuing plans while it watched, in mounting frustration, South Korea's rapid rise in the international economic league to become 'Korea Inc.'; South Korea comfortably fed its growing population while the north tried to hide its constant economic shortfalls. The regime continued to trumpet self-sufficiency while begging for handouts from all and sundry, even the hated Americans. The northern economy also suffered from a number of natural disasters. In 1998 the government began to allow some private ownership and decentralized control over production. A second round of reforms in 2002 tried to produce salaries that people could live on without subsidies and to allow some flexibility in pay and bonuses. And yet a system that originally wanted to ditch money altogether was obviously going to struggle with competitive salaries and then private markets.

Nevertheless, despite the success of local markets and business oligarchs, the country remains in the stubborn grip of a command economy. Money can be made by playing a system that needs to be removed, or at least seriously reformed. When Kim Jong-un took over, the gross national annual income per capita was $1,523 compared with $28,430 in the south. Since then the north has improved a little but the south has gone into overdrive.

Citizens of the DPRK have not paid tax since the early 1970s – they earned very little anyway, as they lived in state housing and survived on food coupons. The small amount of money paid in salaries tended to be for 'luxury' items such as awful movies and cigarettes nearly as bad. Education (often reasonable) and healthcare (very poor) were free until healthcare was paralyzed by the hunger years. A big variety of goods became available in department stores and supermarkets in Pyongyang but this was partly for show to foreigners and partly for the elite. The average Joe had to make do with the *jangmadang.*

Jangmadang were local farmers' markets, selling food, but other small markets sold smuggled goods, often electronic. Many of the market tradespeople were harassed by local jobsworths but often a small bribe could secure permission to trade for a little longer. Most of the traders tended to be women because technically men (under 60) were supposed to be working, often in factories or industries that had long since closed. When the famine started in the early 1990s basic goods, such as rice and vegetables, were sold – sometimes grown in small private plots. It was often a communal effort involving relatives and neighbours especially in the countryside and small towns. Goods were often bartered as few people had any cash in *won*, the national currency, issued by the Central Bank.

As the markets grew in importance and the state left most traders alone most of the time, they started getting more goods and finance for start-ups from relatives or friends across the border in China. The northern superpower became dominant in both informal *and* formal DPRK economies. At the end of the Kim Jong-il era the average monthly salary was around $2 but the average family had to earn a lot more by working in the black economy. Because private transport was rare, the occasional use of a state vehicle for taxis or deliveries was useful, or selling handcraft or home-grown vegetables. As markets boomed so did police bribery to allow the mini-capitalism. As the black market accelerated so did private education not just for the elite but for the army of successful smugglers living near the border. Normally, without party affiliations, they could not get their children into a good-ish school or university. Now traders could make sure that their youngsters could get literally to the front of the class, and secure the full attention of the teachers who also needed the extra money on top of their peanut salaries. Private language instruction flourished as did the sales of music classes as well as computer purchases. By 2017 it was estimated that the DPRK had perhaps over 400 government-approved markets while usually turning a blind eye to the many smaller unofficial enterprises.

Originally the main impulse for the markets was food from local gardens produced by people on tiny plots known as *sotoji* (which means 'small land'); then largescale black-market food imports were coming from China, especially after the harvest season. It also depends on the weather: in 2015, for example, drought tripled the price of potatoes. Markets increased the quantity *and* quality of food available. Besides food, markets would sell rice cookers, cosmetics, DVD-players and the like. Many sellers pretend their goods are made in China or South Korea but they are often DPRK fakes.

Despite the puritanical nature of the regime, drugs became a big part of the market culture. Soft drugs like cannabis as well as amphetamines plus other powerful drugs are one of the ways of coping with a very hard, sometimes brutal, existence. The police are often bribed with regular handouts of drugs. Whether the DPRK has as big a drug problem as the USA is arguable. That said, Pyongyang is one of the safest capitals in the world, especially for foreigners.

Some of the markets involved animals – bringing country life to the towns. Loan sharks and foreign currency dealing, especially in Chinese *yuan*, also proliferate at the markets. As banks have hardly ever functioned in the country the market stalls are the main means of transactions. Taking a loan, perhaps to buy a bicycle or even a motorbike, is also more common. Retired state doctors, struggling on meagre pensions, ply their expertise although most of the clinicians are quacks busy selling traditional Korean herbal medicines.

Some outside experts have suggested that so-called '*Jangmadang* Generation' could bring reform especially as many of the goods come from an obviously far more prosperous China. And some of the imports allow electronic access to the outside world. North Koreans are able to see that their country is almost the poorest, not the richest, in the world. The response of the government has been ambiguous. Police would sometimes crack down on unofficial sellers so that they had to move around – they were dubbed 'grasshopper merchants'. Officials also tried to stop some Chinese imports and attempted to persuade or force people to buy the same goods – at higher prices – in government shops. The government also tried to control the burgeoning private truck business – without trucks the markets are far more difficult to supply. Market vendors are often forced to wear ID cards around their necks to prove they had paid for the pitches. The age of female vendors was also restricted. Previously women under 40 were forbidden although more recently this has been relaxed. Also, theoretically, only retired men, aged over 60, were allowed to trade in the markets. Men tend to run the transport and wholesale side while women, often older women, engage in direct sales. The government appears to have given up on restricting the markets, not least because the attempt, in the last days of the Kim Jong-il period, to stop foreign currency dealing by heavily devaluing the won caused inflation and even protests.

The DPRK still operates a large industrial sector making military equipment, as well as chemical and textile plants. Most important, iron and steel production is one of the success stories for the north and an important foreign exchange earner. The country has also explored oil reserves in its territorial waters. The agricultural co-operatives and state farms had once been successful but poor planning, under-investment and natural disasters – droughts, floods and typhoons – wrecked the farms by the late 1980s. Today agriculture has suffered from fertilizer shortages as well as decrepit machinery; plus much of the soil has been utterly depleted by over-farming and poor terracing on the hills and mountains has caused erosion due to flooding. Commercial fishing has always supplemented land-based food production and, interestingly, Pyongyang has tried to increase its foreign earnings from tourism to new projects such as the Masikryong ski resort.

Masikryong ski resort

This first ski resort was constructed in 2013 as part of Kim Jong-un's drive to increase tourism from 200,000 to one million; around 80 per cent of visitors are from China. The ski resort was built in ten months by the army at a Stakhanovite rate which created the local phrase 'Masikryong speed'. The resort, just twenty miles from the Wonsan port, has nine runs often supplied by snow cannon. It boasts a thirty-year-old Austrian gondola lift that China supplied to Pyongyang; Beijing obviously decided that the international sanctions on luxuries did not include ski lifts.

It is a jarring and long journey on nearly empty roads from the capital, via rice fields, to the new resort. On route, tourists can see that farmers are using ox-drawn ploughs. Hardly a tractor can be seen. The peasants earn very little but foreigners have to pay $150 a night to stay at the ski centre, although there is a discount for North Koreans. Many of the beaches at the nearby Wonsan resort are off-limits to foreigners who are restricted to beaches that are marked 'foreigners only'. The temperatures are roughly the same as Valencia in Spain, which is on the same latitude. Some of old Wonsan town is seedy and crumbling. Pulverized during the Korean War, the strategic port endured the longest naval siege in modern history – 861 days. Later it was the main ferry port for shipping to Japan but Tokyo stopped this smuggling run in 2006. Wonsan has broad streets with colourful billboards with inspiring slogans such as 'Let's advance with the power of science'. Locals own few cars – most ride bicycles. Compared with the ski resort, the local hotel for foreigners has all the charms of the old Soviet bloc, with its intermittent electric and water supply, ropey old towels and very hard beds, though the restaurants appear to be well-provisioned, populated by tourists and locals.[3]

Special Economic Zones
The DPRK has also set up special economic zones along the borders. Initially the SEZs numbered six then they grew to nineteen. Few worked well. An exception was the Kaesong Industrial Region in the south which had a large number of South Korean companies that employed around 50,000 North Korean workers. The DPRK seemed to understand little of modern investment and capitalism. They would change the management rules and pay structures unilaterally and almost arbitrarily. They had numerous rows over rent with the 123 small and medium South Korean firms. Pyongyang charged roughly four times the amount as, for example, the Vietnamese did for South Korean firms investing there. Kaesong was closed unilaterally but temporarily by North Korea in September 2013 though it was later closed permanently by Seoul. In the north, the SEZ in Rason worked reasonably well as it was dominated by Chinese and some Russian businesses.

* * *

The country's energy infrastructure has not been properly maintained and power shortages are endemic. Coal produces most of the energy along with about 17 per cent hydro-electric. Under Kim Jong-un the government worked on renewable energy deploying solar and wind power. The government also claims that it has focused on nuclear plants for energy rather than weapons production but few outside the DPRK believe that.

Transport

The state has 5,200 kilometres of railways operating for passengers and freight; most routes are standard but there are also narrow-gauge lines. The primary rail gateway to North Korea is via the Sino-Korean Friendship Bridge from Dandong, China, to Sinuiju, North Korea. There are several other active border crossings with China, including at Manpo and at Namyang.

Rajin has a rail link to the Russian Railways system over a bridge across the Tumen river. A trans-border passenger service runs from Pyongyang to Moscow, with a Korean rail-car taken across the border (with bogies changed to the Russian gauge), and eventually attached to a Vladivostok-Moscow train. After 2013 the line over the Tumen river to Rajin was rebuilt with dual-gauge track, so that standard-gauge and Russian broad-gauge trains could access the port of Rajin. In 2000, a freight service was inaugurated between South Korea and the industrial park at Kaesong; usage has been very low and most trains carried no freight. Plans for a major north-south rail link never materialized, not least because of military objections, allegedly in the south.

The Metro in the capital is impressive and highly ornate like the Moscow subway. Platforms stand in an elegant floral-themed chamber. There are marble columns designed like plant stems with glass and metal chandeliers fashioned into complicated leaf patterns. The peppermint-green trains are clean.

Many of the roads have not been properly surfaced and are badly maintained. Most people own bicycles but few – besides the elite – own cars. Kim Jong-il disliked women riding cycles, so females on bikes in the cities are rare (though there is a professional national female cycling team). The country is full of contradictions – unpaved roads and peasants on rickety bikes would pass impressive modern scientific institutions.

Communications

The State Academy of Sciences set up over forty research institutes. High tech is important for military development but also for the economy as a whole. Large sums have been poured into the National Aerospace Development Administration. The DPRK was the tenth country to launch a successful satellite – Pyongyang typically overindulged in rhetoric by saying it intended to undertake manned Moon missions. The country has installed a national fibre-optic phone system with nearly two million lines but phones have traditionally been reserved for officials. Mobile phones using a 3G network were set up which proved very popular not least with the *jangmadang* generation. International calls via mobile phones or landlines, as well as the internet, are restricted. You would have to get a Chinese cell phone on the black market, drive to the Chinese border and then even along the way state security officials could stop you. Very few North Koreans are able to go online. The real internet is allowed only for spies, scientists and party elites. The 'walled-garden' state intranet is called *Kwangmyong*. This translates as 'bright light'; unfortunately for North Koreans state controls prevent much light from abroad entering the closed system. State media dominates; some closed academic web sites and an e-mail service operate too.

Media

The Reporters Without Borders' yearly Press Freedom Index awarded the DPRK the very bottom position (180) out of 180 nations. All DPRK media are enslaved to propaganda, and journalists are forced to be tame party members. Listening to broadcasts from outside the country can be punished with severe or even fatal penalties, rather like the Gestapo's monitoring of BBC usage in Nazi-occupied Europe. Security Police regularly check homes to ensure that the TV and radios are not tuned to anything but state media. All the dozen or so major newspapers plus a handful of periodicals are published in Pyongyang. The main national paper, *Rodong Sinmun* (Labour News), is like *Pravda* during the Soviet period, only far more turgid. Three state-controlled TV stations broadcast, two just on the weekends and the other is on every day but only in the evenings. Couch potatoes watching daytime TV have not been a blight, therefore, in the DPRK. Local versions of Twitter and YouTube issued state-controlled pictures and videos.

In 2012 North Korea allowed the Associated Press to open the first fully Western news bureau in the highly secretive country. The north had permitted foreign media on occasional visits, often for important ceremonial occasions, although journalists were restricted in their movements and accompanied by usually two official minders (presumably to snoop on each other as well). The press minders are very fussy about the numerous statues of the leaders around the country. Ever paranoid, there had been a campaign to alert locals to the possibilities of South Korean or American spies trying to blow up the monuments to the great leaders. The very few Western TV camera operators allowed are always instructed to avoid filming from the rear or the side of statues – they have to be filmed in proper context and in full screen. Otherwise it is showing great disrespect to the great leaders

The new AP bureau was housed in the offices of the Korean Central News Agency. The government also controlled some of the staff employment, including reportedly two secret policemen. The bureau was constantly accused of pulling its punches and not reporting on major stories such as the six-week disappearance of Kim Jong-un that was a big story in outside Asian papers. Most egregiously, the AP did not report at all on the big international story about the DPRK hacking Sony because of the film, *The Interview*.

Nevertheless films such as *The Interview* as well as perceived saucy movies such as, er, *Charlie's Angels*, have been smuggled in as DVDs. Despite Kim Jong-il's obsession with movie-making the standard of local production has been poor, mainly based on historic events or folk tales. They have not been popular with their largely captive audiences but are arguably better than the old Soviet love stories about boy meets tractor. The elite watch practically anything they so desire. Sometimes popular Western films are shown to university students as an example of Western decadence. *Titanic* was screened extensively, presumably on the ideological grounds of displaying greedy capitalists living decadent lives and then grabbing all the lifeboats.

The stifling control of the media has meant that often lurid stories, frequently generated from right-wing papers in South Korea, gained real credibility. Did Kim Jong-un really undergo surgery to look like his grandfather? Did young Kim execute his girlfriend and did he really feed his uncle to a pack of starving dogs or, another version, tear him apart personally with anti-aircraft fire? The first two stories are almost certainly disinformation – 'fake news'. In the last case, Kim Jong-un's uncle was probably shot by a military firing squad. The danger with such Orwellian control has been that most rumours, no matter how outlandish – and North Korean events are frequently surreal – have been believed. Pyongyang's regular effusions of official disinformation have added to the enigma that is the DPRK.

That is the challenge of complete control – which even respectable Western agencies such as AP can confirm. The AP pioneers soon led the way for AFP – Agence France-Presse; the Kyoko Japanese agency as well as Russian and Chinese news companies joined in. Some information flexibility for the foreign – if not the domestic media – does suggest some *political* flexibility in Kim Jong-un's allegedly fresh approach.

For decades the word 'reform' was taboo – it implied that the system was not perfect. The old system just had to be made to work properly. The people just had to work harder and had to implement the leadership's decisions more thoroughly. Kim Jong-un's tolerance of some markets brought more food and an improvement in lifestyles. As all authoritarian regimes have discovered, slight loosening of repression is when the cracks become chasms in the social structure. In Eastern Europe, marketization brought political reform. As Russian scholar and Korea expert Andrei Lankov put it, 'While filling the people's bellies with food, the government will have to continue to fill their people's hearts with fear.'

Lankov may be correct and yet regime survival may depend on the simple ability of the regime to feed the military and Pyongyang's elite. In a country long racked by famine, food may be more important than democracy. You can't eat democracy. South Sudan is the most recent example of this truism.

Chapter 7

Daily Life

The single most important feature in the life in the DPRK has always been the ubiquity of the ruling dynasty. A defector, a North Korean doctor, said: 'It's like a religion. From your birth you learn that the Kim family are gods, and you are taught to be utterly obedient to them. It's a reign of terror. The Kim family uses terror to keep people scared.'[1] Many dictatorships have adopted the motto of the Roman emperors and Machiavelli: that it is better, and safer, for the rulers to be feared than loved. The classic is *Oderint dum metuant:* let them hate me as long as they fear me. But the Kims needed to be loved as well as totally obeyed. Failure to do so was often fatal.

Kim Il-sung wanted to build not only a new country but to create a new breed of better people, *socialist* better people. Man not God would shape the fate of each citizen. They were being controlled ultimately for their own good, their own happiness.

A sarcastic inflection when referring to Kim Il-sung or a nostalgic remark about South Korea or Japan could get someone into deep trouble. A real taboo is to question who actually started the Korean War. It is always best to keep your mouth shut. That applies especially if you are a Christian or a member of the perceived 'hostile' class.

The previous chapter examined the caste system (*Sonbung*) that has controlled nearly all aspects of daily life, though it has been modified, a little, for most people by some green shoots of capitalism. The party and security organs also wield the whip where custom and caste may fail. The worst fate is imprisonment in one of the six main labour camps for political prisoners. Both public and secret executions of inmates, including children, especially in the case of attempted escape, were common. Many of the possibly 200,000 prisoners died from starvation, work accidents and torture. One prison guard at Camp 22, Ahn Myong-Chol, admitted that they had been trained to treat the prisoners as subhuman, as in the Nazi death camps and Japanese PoW camps. He gave one account of children who fought over bits of corn retrieved from cow droppings.[2]

In a previous chapter the various kinds of camps were examined. The camps for political prisoners have always been much harsher. These internment camps, located in the centre and north-east of the DPRK, were usually built in isolated mountain valleys. Most inmates expect to be there for life, while some lesser offences might offer the chance of eventual parole. The prisoners usually work in mines or on the land as slave labourers using primitive tools. The food rations are tiny, so an estimated 40 per cent have died from malnutrition. Those who survive are often crippled by work accidents, torture or frostbite. Stealing food or trying to escape were punished by public execution.

Kang Chol-hwan, from ethnic Korean stock who had lived in Japan, was an inmate of Yodok Prison Camp. He survived and managed to get out of the country and, after finding God, wrote a moving book called *The Aquariums of Pyongyang*. As a young boy, he was imprisoned along with the rest of his family when his grandfather was incarcerated for suspected anti-government activities. For ten years his whole family suffered disease, starvation and torture. One of the sensational aspects of the book was the claim that the national football team members were locked up after the 1966 World Cup because of a perceived poor performance. The footballers have denied this – well, they would, wouldn't they? The offending grandfather died after ten years and his family was released. Kang Chol-hwan escaped to China and later managed to reach South Korea.[3]

Most citizens are too cowed by the state punishments of so many people that they try to keep their heads down and conform. Part of the conformity comes instinctively from effective brainwashing, starting with school. Even very young children are taught to hate 'America'. The USA is referred to as 'the eternal enemy with whom we can never co-exist under the same sky'. Just as in Orwell's ritual in *1984* – The Two Minutes of Hate – children boo at Americans in propaganda films and are even encouraged to throw things at the screen. Schools are organized on military lines with uniforms, parades and ranks. Even at the top universities the military structures and training are important.

At universities students are forbidden to date; those who risk it can be expelled. Physical checks for men and women are held regularly. Females also have gynaecological examinations too to assure the party that they are still virgins. The government line was that women should marry at 20 and men at 28 but few follow that rule strictly now.

Life for women is very restricted by custom and communist rules. For example, hair styles are controlled. Women are not permitted to dye their hair, although perms are common among married women. It is not true that Korean men have to have the same hairstyle as the great leaders: the bouffant in the case of Kim Jong-il or high-side cuts in the manner of the current Kim. Deploying the Kim Jong-un style has not ever been compulsory but it is a handy way of displaying loyalty and maybe creating one less opportunity for security personnel to stop you. Short hair for men has been compulsory, though a range of recommended hairstyles are to be found on the barbers' walls. The party would often issue edicts about hair lengths – longer hair smacked of hippy capitalism. Technically, men could grow hair no longer than five centimetres on top though an exception was made for balding men (they were allowed seven centimetres) so they could implement a comb-over.

Fashion is very conservative; even the earth-shattering very late emergence of the bikini included a little skirt. But Ri Sol-ju, Kim Jong-un's glamorous wife, has both rejuvenated the leadership and humanized her husband. She has been compared with the role of Kate Middleton in the British royal family.[4] Like Kim Jong-un's mother, the current first lady was a performer in a travelling troupe. Nevertheless she comes from a good political family in that her father served in a senior position in the air force.

Individuals have been subjected to constant surveillance. The most fear and irritation have probably been generated by the *inminban*, usually a middle-aged female busybody who runs the neighbourhood watch in, say, a group of thirty to forty families. North Koreans joke that the *inminban* is supposed to know how many spoons and chopsticks each family own. They practise all sorts of petty snooping, from checking that no-one was watching TV when the state channel(s) has finished and so were indulging in smuggled videos. TVs and radios are sold pre-set so that they receive only official channels. But there are ways around this, not least with contraband from China. The *inminban* also keeps a beady eye on possible affairs of the heart. The state has always taken a dim view of pre-marital or extra-marital sex. For example, a little dalliance at work can result in group criticism and public humiliation for both man and woman, plus a possible demotion or sacking. Traditionally marriages are arranged by families and party officials. Pregnancy outside marriage is a very shameful rarity in a society where women do not smoke in public, let alone flirt. In more recent years the state has begun to turn a blind eye to some sexual shenanigans – but only heterosexual ones. 'The only gay in the village' in the English catchphrase would mean the only gay in the whole country in the DPRK. Many gays did not even understand the term until they had defected and discovered that another sexuality existed. Gays were occasionally executed but the penal code does not mention even the possibility of such behaviour. It simply does not feature in the correct socialist lifestyle. In 2009 the penal code was altered to include a possible reference to the LGBT community – 'decadent' behaviour or culture. Pyongyang should not be included in the top gay tourist destinations, therefore.

Spying on one's own countrymen became a national pastime, a little like the Securitate operations in Romania or the Stasi in East Germany. Vigilantes from the Socialist Youth League might stop people for infringements such as not wearing the omnipresent leadership lapel badges. They also stopped people for wearing blue jeans or T-shirts with Roman lettering – both capitalist indulgences. Mobile police units would roam the streets looking for social offenders; they have the right to walk into people's homes without notice. (They would ostentatiously never remove their shoes, a standard Korean sign of respect.) They might fine people for using a light bulb of more than 40 watts. They can check on guests who are visiting to see if they have proper travel permits. And besides such official bodies, because the country does not have the electronic systems or the electricity for sophisticated surveillance, it all comes down to individuals to protect the fatherland against subversive behaviour. The society is crammed full of busybodies, jobsworths and snoopers. The newspapers often run stories about heroic and patriotic children ratting on a possible off-hand remark by one of their own parents.

Music is played everywhere – especially telling people to work harder and aspire to follow the great leaders. In lifts (when they work) and public spaces it is hard to escape. But the most ubiquitous sign of loyalty in North Korea is the party badge that everyone wears, regardless of whether they are party members or not. After you are 14 you put one on. The small badge showing the first two leaders is always worn on the left, over the heart.

North Koreans queue as well as the British, except that it is not first come first served. Far from it. Traditionally there are three signs for three queues: cadres, military personnel and ordinary residents. Party members waiting for trains use a separate and relatively comfortable waiting room. North Koreans have no freedom to travel. To buy a ticket you have to get a travel pass that states the reason for travel. If you are caught travelling without a pass, it usually means three months of hard labour. Special passes with a red line across the top (very like the secret or classified documents used in the UK) are insisted on for travel in the areas near the capital, and the border areas with China or South Korea. These special passes are also issued with a secret, time-limited code. Security checkpoints are set up on all roads that cross the internal borders of counties and provinces, even up in the hills.

The most crucial regimentation, especially during the pre-Kim Jong-un period, was the food rationing. Before it collapsed it allocated a daily ration, which supplied food and household goods such as cooking oil. This was issued to senior party personnel. There were successively fewer locations called three-day rations, weekly rations and monthly rations.

Jang Jin-sung was one of 'The Admitted'. That meant that he had been specially favoured by the Dear Leader, Kim Jong-il – in his case for his literary work. Because of this and his government propaganda job in Pyongyang – he used to forge pro-regime literary works by imaginary South Korean writers – he had no shortage of food. But he went to a provincial town to visit old school friends. In his book, *Dear Leader* (page 51), he described the conditions of former friends 'who had turned into nothing but skin and bones. Their prematurely darkened cavernous skin and deep zigzagging wrinkles on their faces were a silent testament to the years of starvation they had endured.'

In contrast, the capital of North Korea became one large Potemkin village. Selected party loyalists live, work and study there, not least because it is considered a showcase to the world. Life in the countryside has been banned to nearly all foreigners (except some NGOs such as the Red Cross), so conditions have to be analysed via the testimony of defectors and refugees. Obviously many of these former North Koreans have an axe to grind.

One of the constant themes of Barbara Demick's revealing book about the DPRK lifestyle, *Nothing to Envy,*[5] was the only way young people could meet secretly – by moving around in the dark and walking and talking unseen in quiet areas. Maybe they even held hands. Foreign analysts always mention the curious lack of lighting shown in satellite photography of the DPRK, a black hole next to glittering areas of Japan, China and South Korea. The blank space, the size of England, is the DPRK. Electricity for home or work is often in short supply. South Korea is lit up because it has billboards, car lights and the neon of fast-food joints plus every building, domestic dwellings or work-place is illuminated. Until the recent smuggling of USBs, DVDs and Chinese phones with internet access near the border, many North Koreans had no idea of how prosperous nearly every other society was, especially the prosperity of South Korea. The division of the peninsula is not like the partition of Germany. There is no postal communication between the two, let alone phone or e-mail connections. The DPRK is dark and isolated. Life is grey. (Again the capital is different: many of the big housing projects are painted in colourful washes – pink, rose red and pale blue.)

Most housing blocks in the towns and villages were monochromatic as well as being basic and utilitarian. Little traditional housing survived the destruction of the Korean War. The new stock was built in the 1960s and 1970s from cement blocks and limestone often given to the people and based on their rank and job. In the urban areas the state organized so-called 'pigeon coops', small units in low-rise apartment blocks. In the countryside people used to live in what were nicknamed 'harmonicas' – rows and rows of single-room boxes that looked a bit like a mouth organ. Often up to a dozen families might share a bathroom. Until recently, especially in the rural areas, only half the population had flushing lavatories. In the harmonicas, occasionally the odd hedonist might paint the front door a bright colour but otherwise the colour is grey or sometimes whitewashed. Just as in George Orwell's dystopia, Big Brother permitted colour only in massive propaganda posters. In North Korea the great leaders loom large in lurid colours painted in the socialist realism style.

Somehow, through all the oppression, security police harassment and hunger, people survived, adapted and coped – many died, however. In the 1990s while South Korea was becoming the world's largest exporter of mobile telephones, most North Koreans had never used a phone. You had to queue at a post office to make a call. For years paper was in short supply, so writing a letter was not that easy either.

Life has improved, especially in the capital but even in 2019 it is still tough for all who are not in the business, party or military elites. Electricity cuts are still endemic and even in the capital the lack of heating means that people sleep in layers of clothing in the winter. But families, although small, are not restricted in size as they were until recently in China. Most women use a coil as contraceptive. Women have improved their status, not least because of their increased role as breadwinners in markets. (Traditionally in Korea women have managed household finances.) Also the new high-profile roles of the leader's wife and sister have raised female aspirations.

An interesting aside is the slight change in language towards women. The complex Korean language has a large array of verb endings that vary according to the status of the speaker or audience. Two of the most common levels are the 'honorific speech' used for speaking respectfully to a superior or using plain speech when talking to social inferiors or children. (This is common in old traditional languages; for example in Welsh it is common to address children and pets in the familiar form of the verb – cf French: tu instead of vous.) North Korean women use the honorific form when addressing men, who in turn use plain speech when replying. This has gone in South Korea and now is beginning to be eroded in the north. For a foreigner in the DPRK it is not a bad idea to use the honorific with women, not just because it is polite and is appreciated but because it is a far simpler form to learn.[6]

North Koreans have a little more leisure time and things to do. Although many of the parades and synchronized dancing may seem odd to a foreign eye, mostly North Koreans take pride in their children practising for such (very competitive) events put on for state holidays and events. And adults enjoy the communal informal dancing (often in traditional dress) as well as singing in parks during the popular picnics. The most common form of relaxation, however, is just chatting with friends and family over tea or sometimes *soju* (the often powerful rocket fuel-cum-hooch). Drunkenness among men is common, especially in the local equivalent of Karaoke bars, but women's heavy drinking is not tolerated. Families also enjoy watching DVDs at home; its technical illegality probably spices up the pleasure of watching South Korean soaps. People seem too busy to read for pleasure, even Korean fiction; anyway, contemporary novels in translation are hard to find. Basketball is very popular as is volleyball.

Food supplies are better, especially in the capital. But ordinary North Koreans will tend to eat rice and *kimche* (spiced pickled cabbage) a lot, with some bean stew. Meat is not eaten regularly. And the diet, even when food is abundantly available, tends to be monotonous. Foreigners can find some reasonable restaurants in the main towns, especially near the Chinese border, in Wonsan and in Pyongyang. Dog meat is considered a treat but is not usually served to foreigners. Visitors to North Korea usually comment that they don't see many cats and dogs. One of the reasons is that they have to be fed and in the hunger years humans were dying for lack of food. The party used to discourage animals as pets as they were considered unhealthy, but now the elite have dogs and, of course, dog-walkers.

To an outsider, North Korean life was and is unbearable but it needs repeating that many North Koreans pride themselves on their stoical adaptation. Even those who secretly hate the regime still take pride in the country's resilience. As numerous interviews with defectors confirm, many still celebrate North Korea's successes, perhaps in sport for example, or even in the independent nuclear deterrent – forged at such great costs to individual lifestyles. Even after risking all by fleeing the country, it is hard for some not to feel some pride, refugees say, in the fact that a small country has stood up to the world's most powerful nation, the USA. The North Koreans are a patriotic people almost regardless of the state brainwashing.

Chapter 8

On the Front Line: South Korea

The savagery of the Korean War entrenched the military dictatorships in both north and south, except that the Republic of South Korea eventually grew out of (some of) its authoritarianism, partly because of American tutelage as well as rapid economic development. (China, however, has proved – so far – that one-party control can march alongside rapid economic progress.) The south held relatively free elections in 1987, it is true, and despite extensive corruption other relatively free elections ensued. But many voters in the south became increasingly weary of the highly personalized and faction-ridden political process. And Seoul seemed incapable of taking effective action against the might of the big commercial conglomerates, the *chaebol*. Increasingly, younger voters who had no memory of American support against the Japanese and then the 1950 invasion were becoming less pro-American, especially after various incidents in which South Korean civilians had been killed accidentally by US military vehicles. In 2003 restaurants started showing signs saying that Americans were not welcome.

Although both Korean states claim all of the Korean peninsula, both joined the UN and were recognized by most other member states. Dialogue between the two was inevitable – not least to reduce the chronic tensions and for genuine reasons of cultural coherence in one of the most homogenous of all peoples. And yet Pyongyang announced six times between 1994 and 2013 that it would no longer abide by the armistice – in short, threatening to return to war. In Seoul the north's 'sea of fire' threats were taken seriously. Just a few miles north of Seoul, over the border, the North Korean army maintained between 8,000 and 10,000 rocket-launchers and long-range guns; they could fire up to 300,000 shells an hour on to the southern capital or other population centres.

It was estimated that up to a million Koreans had been separated from immediate family members by the fighting and so part of Seoul's policy was to assist family reunions, as well as to reduce military friction. Talking had begun in earnest in the 1970s but it was on-off – the default style of Pyongyang's manipulative diplomacy. In 2000 Kim Dae-jung, the southern leader, became the first president of the Republic of South Korea to visit the north – fifty-five years after the great powers had divided the country.

Both countries competed to prove their economic virility, a contest clearly won by the south. After the 1950–53 war, South Korea emerged as one of the twentieth century's most amazing economic success stories, becoming a developed, globally connected, high-tech society within decades. In the 1960s GDP per capita was comparable with levels in the poorest countries in the world. By 2004 South Korea had joined the trillion-dollar club of international economies. No wonder the DPRK has done everything it could to stop its citizens from viewing TV and films from the south. The differences between the hermit kingdom's directed economy and the freewheeling capitalism of the south are profound. Sometimes, however, the competition is merely petty. The construction of Pyongyang's elegant Metro, for example, spurred on a replica – but better, it was claimed – in Seoul. They also competed over the height of their respective flagpoles in the occasional meeting place of Panmunjom.

South Korea's economy surpassed that of its neighbour many times over. The north's GDP was estimated to be $40 billion in 2015, while that of the south was $1.92 trillion for the same period. And most North Korean statistics are extremely suspect and usually exaggerated. According to the *CIA Handbook*, the contribution to GDP in 2017 in the north by agriculture, industry and services was estimated at 22.5 per cent, 47.6 per cent, and 29.9 per cent respectively while in the south it was 2.2 per cent, 39.3 per cent, and 58.3 per cent. South Korea's became the world's eleventh largest economy in terms of GDP. Seoul could boast of world-famous brands such as Samsung and Hyundai. Despite its uneven democracy in the past and corruption in the present, Korea faced many problems in the future, not least a stalling growth rate, youth unemployment and poverty among the ageing population. These were challenges faced, however, in many advanced economies.

The military tensions over the DMZ undermined both sides. President Bill Clinton described the four-kilometre-wide strip as 'the scariest place on earth'. The Democratic president tried hard to engage with North Korea in the 1990s and helped with food aid (usually 300,000 tonnes annually) as well as fuel and technical assistance with civilian nuclear energy. Nevertheless, the DMZ could have been the trip-wire for nuclear war at almost any time. North Korea's *Juche* policy of self-reliance and *songun*, the military-first imperative, completely skewed the northern economy. Sanctions didn't help either, although aid from the UN and immense largesse from the Chinese partly compensated. The north suffered, too, from the collapse of the USSR and then natural disasters. Gradually, Chinese aid and investment and the formation of Special Economic Zones on the border started to give the Kim Jong-un regime a chance to compete. The north's infrastructure was backward and its economy ossified by red tape but it did have lots of unexplored natural resources estimated to be worth trillions of dollars – one of the reasons why Russia and China continue to embrace North Korea.

In the final analysis the fundamental issues are war and peace and whether unification is possible. As usual, inter-Korean relations have been tied to great-power manoeuvres. Secret talks between Seoul and Pyongyang were arranged at the same time as President Richard Nixon's overtures to the Chinese in 1971–72. In August 1971 the first Red Cross talks were held between both sides. Top Korean intelligence chiefs met regularly and sometimes they were productive. An example was the July 1972 'principles on re-unification' – resolution of the division of one people should be done peacefully and without interference from outside powers. A 'hotline' – so fashionable in the Cold War – was established.

Despite most Koreans' innate xenophobia, not least about how to achieve re-unification, a good man who tried to do good for everybody, President Jimmy Carter, had tried to bring both sides together but his plans were derailed because he suggested the withdrawal of US troops. Sometimes Pyongyang seemed highly rational – at other times contradictory or inexplicable. In 1983 a North Korean proposal for talks with Washington and Seoul was scuppered by the apparent North Korean attempt to assassinate the South Korean president in Rangoon. Usually aid went north but in September 1984 Pyongyang sent emergency supplies to the south after severe floods. Talks were resumed and the first reunion of a small number of separated families resulted. But the temporary goodwill collapsed with the US-South Korean (*Hoguk*) military exercises in 1986. Pyongyang always hated these regular exercises because the massive display of military firepower (often near the DMZ) looked suspiciously like a preparation for invasion, especially to the paranoid northerners.

When Seoul was chosen to host the 1988 summer Olympics, North Korea tried to organize a boycott by its various communist allies. The alternative was for north and south to co-host the games, said Pyongyang. The failure of North Korea in the Olympics ploy was assumed by the south to be the reason for the revenge of bringing down Korean Air Flight 858 in 1987.

The downing of Flight 858

A Korean Air Boeing 707 took off from Baghdad International Airport on 29 November 1987 en route to Seoul, but it exploded in mid-air. A bomb had been placed in the overhead lockers by two passengers who had got off in a stop-over in Abu Dhabi. The two disembarking passengers were very highly trained North Korean operatives. All the 104 passengers (mostly South Korean construction workers who had been employed in the Middle East) as well as eleven crew members, perished. Ironically, the sixteen-year-old Boeing 707 had just been painted in new livery with a special addition to promote the forthcoming Olympic games.

The two terrorists, a man and a woman, were tracked down in Bahrain but, just before they were arrested, they swallowed two cyanide capsules hidden in their cigarettes. The male North Korean saboteur died but the woman, Kim Hyun-hee, survived. She was extradited to South Korea but was later pardoned by the president, Roh Tae-woo, because it was accepted that she had been brainwashed in the north. And it was useful politically: during her trial she implicated directly the future northern leader, Kim Jong-il. The downing of the plane was part of the reason that Washington placed North Korea on its list of state sponsors of terrorism.

Because the female bomber published a book on her experiences, the details of the story became well-known.[1] The two saboteurs had travelled via a circuitous route on forged Japanese passports, posing as tourists. Two other North Korean agents gave them the time-bomb, disguised as a Panasonic radio, when they travelled through Vienna. At Saddam

International Airport in Baghdad they planted their bomb in the locker above their seats (7B and 7C) on the Korean Air flight. Later, while flying over the Andaman Sea, the timer set off the separate liquid explosives disguised as a liquor bottle.

The bombers had left the plane at Abu Dhabi airport. Their original escape route was via Jordan, but they were confronted with visa problems and so were forced to fly to Bahrain. Then they had intended to fly to Rome. The customs officials in Bahrain were on the ball and identified the Japanese passports as forgeries. The male operative died from the cyanide but his 25-year-old companion was saved. In Seoul, during her interrogation, she claimed she was a Chinese orphan who had grown up in Japan – her official cover story. She claimed she had no connection with the terror attack. The innocent orphan Annie story was less than convincing, however, because in Bahrain she had attacked a police officer and had tried to seize his gun. During her lengthy interrogation in Seoul she was shown a film about life in the south – and she was utterly amazed to see that it was not the starving and corrupt American puppet she had been told about. Thereupon she threw herself into the arms of one of the female investigators and confessed to everything.

She explained that when she was 16 she had been chosen by the party for a special role and she learned a number of Asian languages, especially Japanese and Mandarin. She was also very beautiful, tough physically and highly intelligent; she was very charming despite her shyness. Men could not resist her, a perfect female agent. After this she underwent training for three years at an espionage school run by the army. Kim Hyun-hee then worked on weapons training and unarmed combat, often coming out with almost perfect marks in her field tests. She also suffered years of physical and psychological conditioning. She explained that she had been personally ordered to bomb the plane by Kim Jong-il, an action which she was told would re-unify her country as well as frighten away competitors from the Olympics to be held in the south. She expressed remorse which may have been genuine as the royalties for her later book (and film) were paid to the families of the victims. She also claimed that Kim Jong-il was behind the attempted assassination of the South Korean president in Rangoon in 1983. Sentenced to death, she was later pardoned by President Roh Tae-woo. He said: 'The persons who ought to be on trial here are the leaders of North Korea .... This child is as much a victim of this evil regime as the passengers aboard KAL 858.' After the initial publicity Kim Hyun-hee, another defector who found God, was forced to live in a secret location to avoid revenge attacks from agents who had undergone training similar to her own.

And, for the record, North Korea insisted that it had nothing to do with the destruction of the airliner.

Cold War Thaw

Despite the north's terrorism and secret raids by the south, both sides were inevitably influenced by the thaw in the Cold War that led to the fall of the Berlin Wall and the implosion of the Soviet Union. And more northerners were finding methods of fleeing to the south, usually via China, just as more and more Eastern Europeans had found ways around the Berlin Wall and various mini-DMZs along the old iron curtain. Both Korean sides had talked endlessly of unification and mostly meant it. The question was how? On whose terms? Gradually, the means seemed more and more peaceful – and not the potential invasion conjured up both in Seoul and Pyongyang. The north had peddled various schemes to create a 'Korean Community' via a form of confederation. President Roh Tae-woo emulated West Germany's *Ostpolitik* with a Korean initiative nicknamed *Nordpolitik*. In September 1990 high-level officials met to try to normalize and demilitarize the peninsula and this coincided with the admission of both states to the UN. A special unification flag was designed and used for the joint Korean table tennis championships in Japan and a youth football competition in Portugal.

In 1991 the US removed all its nukes from South Korea although nuclear-capable warships and aircraft still visited the south. Much later, in 2004, it was discovered that, under pressure from the International Atomic Energy Authority, South Korean scientists admitted that they had enriched uranium secretly in 1979–81, separated small quantities of plutonium in 1982, experimented with uranium enrichment again in 2000 and manufactured depleted-uranium munitions in the mid-1980s. This was small beer compared with the north but if the Seoul government and Washington really did not know it did show a curious lack of interest compared with their scrutiny of what the northerners were up to.

By 2010 South Korea was operating twenty-four nuclear power reactors that met 40 per cent of the country's domestic electricity needs and it was scheduled to expand to around 56 per cent by 2020. South Korea became a major exporter of civilian nuclear power facilities; its first big deal was in 2009 with the United Arab Emirates. By 2030 Seoul planned to sell eighty reactors worth $400 billion, making it the third largest nuclear power exporter. Washington had controlled fuel-cycle techniques in South Korea. Japan, however, had significant processing capabilities but Washington had not allowed the same leeway to Seoul. The USA was aware that granting Seoul the right to reprocess spent fuel would complicate long-term hopes for de-nuclearizing the peninsula as well as antagonize China, besides undermining general anti-proliferation strategies.

A desire for parity with Japan motivated Seoul's requests although the arguments were couched in economic and technical terms. Despite South Korea's insistence that the dual-use nuclear technologies would only be used for peaceful purposes, and that Washington should trust its old ally, the USA could not ignore the growing demands in some South Korean circles that the beleaguered nation should possess its own nukes in response to constant provocations from the DPRK.

*   *   *

Hopes of re-unification went in waves that regularly enveloped the public imagination in South Korea. In late 1991 agreements were finalized about prior notice of major military movements. And, inevitably, discussions followed of transforming the long and uneasy – and very volatile – armistice into a proper peace agreement. Real deals would have to involve the great powers, especially China and the USA. Yet at the same time both north and south felt genuinely, and had to prove publicly, that they were not totally in hock to their big allies. Much could and should be done *a deux*.

These moves towards peace were dubbed the sunshine policy – publicly advocated by the South Korean president, Kim Dae-jung. This led to a summit between the southern president and Kim Jong-il. More family reunions followed (usually 100 families from both sides) and northern and southern teams marched together at the 2000 Sydney Olympics. Just as ping-pong had helped ease US-China détente so sport was deployed by the two Koreas. Trade between the two increased; the Kaesong Industrial Region was set up to allow southern businesses to invest in the north. President Kim Dae-jung also received the Nobel Peace Prize in 2000 for his reconciliation efforts. (Sadly Kaesong closed in 2016 and the countries almost went to war in 2017.)

Washington was now deeply suspicious of the sunshine policy, however. The change of American attitudes was obvious in the transition from the more liberal Democratic policy under Clinton to the harder line under the Republican George W. Bush. In 2002 North Korea was included in George W. Bush's 'axis of evil' because of the growing nuclear weapons potential of the north. When President Bush visited Seoul in early 2002 he contradicted the sunshine policy by stating that he could not trust a leader who starved his own people. And during a visit to the DMZ he consciously emulated Ronald Reagan's call for the Soviet Union 'to tear down the Berlin Wall'. In South Korea Bush told the north to remove all the barbed wire and allow free access to both sides.

After the invasion of Iraq, Washington announced it was going to reduce its military commitment in South Korea by around 12,500 troops. Many in Seoul viewed this decision (later largely rescinded) as a reaction to a wave of anti-Americanism in South Korea rather than as a necessary security adjustment because of US overstretch. Seoul did not want to weaken the alliance, however: South Korea sent 3,500 combat troops and military engineers to Iraq in 2004 on top of the 670 soldiers sent in mid-2003. This was despite criticism from the parliamentary opposition in Seoul. (Japan also committed a similar total troop contingent to Iraq.)

Another constant factor in US-South Korean military relations has been cost-sharing. The costs of US deployment were high, plus there was the argument over the environmental clean-up of relocated American bases. In December 2006 an agreement was reached that increased Seoul's costs by about 6 per cent to approximately $790 million annually. Yet, according to the US Department of Defense, this was just 15 per cent of the total annual costs of maintaining American forces in South Korea.

Many US experts felt that South Korea's booming economy should have permitted far more in contributions to its own defence – just as Donald Trump later argued that the uber-rich German state should offer more for its contribution to NATO.

*   *   *

Despite President George W. Bush's muscular policy in the Middle East, he did try to talk to the North Koreans. Iraq's 'axis' leaders could be destroyed – but that was more difficult with China's neighbour. So a policy sometimes dubbed 'hawkish engagement' was manufactured. At the turn of the millennium the USA had been giving some 500,000 tonnes of heavy fuel oil worth nearly $60 million to North Korea. Under the Agreed Framework Washington was committed to do so until the completion of the first of two light-water reactors to make sure the nuclear advances were for civilian energy and not weapons. The USA also still provided food aid. Having previously been dependent on the USSR and China, Pyongyang began to improve relations with Western Europe and the USA. Of course North Korea maintained 'its spiritual independence by remaining critical of those who feed the country', to quote a 2000 report by London's International Institute of Strategic Studies.

Food shortages had often been a prompt for a dash for freedom. A steady stream of defectors still escaped via China and, to a lesser extent, Russia but it did not become a flood – partly because it was so difficult and dangerous, as the whole extended family of any escapee or would-be escaper would be severely punished. (A handful still went the other way, from south to north.) Sometimes the Chinese would return groups of escapers to their grisly fate in North Korea. Seoul was often in two minds about this. The ROK government had no wish to absorb a flood of poorly qualified North Korean refugees who would find it difficult to adapt to the thrust of capitalist life in the south. On the other hand, some defectors came with a wealth of useful data, especially if they had senior positions in the regime.

The tough Bush foreign policy exacerbated strains between Washington and Seoul. Obviously North Korea was a threat to democratic free market economies in both countries but the 2006 *Strategic Survey* of the International Institute for Strategic Studies summarized the different perceptions thus:

> Where Americans see an increasingly dangerous and repressive regime, South Koreans see a pitiable renegade brother, estranged by an accident of history in which America was culpable. South Koreans do not believe that North Koreans would use their nuclear weapons unless they were forced to do so for regime survival. South Koreans are thus more afraid of a US policy of regime change that could provoke North Korea.

Seoul was always more concerned with stability on the peninsula than North Korean human rights. South Korea feared that Washington's explicit attacks on this front would undermine its engagement strategy. In addition, Seoul's increasing eagerness to invest and trade with the north obviously contradicted Washington's policy of applying financial pressures. Joint industrial parks seemed the way forward to Seoul, not welcoming a prominent North Korean defector (Kang Chol-hwan, the author of *The Aquariums of Pyongyang*) to the White House as President Bush did in June 2006. Seoul was not concerned with commercial issues alone: South Korea wanted to keep pace with Beijing's economic embrace of the north as part of its strategy to control the peninsula. Seoul wanted a united country along the lines of its existing free-market model. The South Korean government knew that Beijing had no interest in allowing a Western-orientated unified Korea on its border. Moreover, Seoul had no desire to be enlisted in an anti-Chinese strategic alliance. South Koreans did not want to be dragged into a war in Asia 'against the will of the Korean people'. For example, Seoul worried that US forces, including ones based in South Korea, would become embroiled in a fight over Taiwan.

Seoul sisters: US–South Korean animosities

South Korea remains one of the most pro-American countries in the world and yet beneath the numerous political and military connections a deep seam of suspicion lingers. And some of it goes back a long way. The destruction of the American ship *General Sherman* in 1866 and the major punitive expedition in 1871 had painted the USA as an intrusive and aggressive power. In July 1905 US Secretary of War William Howard Taft reached an understanding with Katsura Taro, the prime minister of Japan. It was neither a signed agreement, nor a secret treaty but it has inspired much historical debate. The Taft-Katsura discussions have been interpreted by some critics of Washington as a deal whereby the US recognized Korea as part of the Japanese sphere of influence while the Philippines were accepted as part of the American sphere. Even before direct US involvement in the Korean War, many Koreans, north and south, intensely disliked the American habit of ignoring local opinion and local political organizations. Likewise, many in both Koreas have blamed Washington for cynically bisecting the country with Moscow. Americans also had a habit of relying on Japanese collaborators and not nationalists in the early days of South Korea. Far worse was the antipathy caused by a number of US atrocities from 1950 to 1953, especially the shooting of civilians. The North Korean forces did have a policy of infiltrating their troops into civilian refugee movements, however. Civilians were also killed in indiscriminate artillery and bombing raids. Hundreds of South Korean civilians were killed by the US 7th Cavalry Regiment and the USAF in July 1950 at a railway bridge near the village of No Gun Ri. Perhaps as many as 400 men, women and children were killed – though estimates vary. Along with My Lai in former South Vietnam, it is considered one of the largest single massacres of civilians by US troops in the twentieth century. South Korean historians have accused the Americans of a large number of other atrocities, albeit with fewer casualties.

The DPRK's propaganda has claimed much bigger atrocities by the Americans, such as 35,000 civilians killed in late 1950 at Sinchon but little evidence has been offered by Pyongyang. The north claimed that between 17 October and 7 December South Korean forces, under the command of the US, committed the abominations during the retreat of DPRK armies from Hwanghae. The figure of 35,000 was about one quarter of the population of Sinchon at the time. Northern propaganda in schools has taught that Americans 'hammered nails into victims' heads' and 'sliced off women's breasts'. The propaganda also claimed that American troops beheaded, with samurai swords, up to 300 civilians. The war museum in Sinchon is a shrine of anti-Americanism.

After the war was paused in 1953 some Koreans continued to blame Washington for the lack of progress on re-unification. During the 1980s arsonists attacked a number of American cultural centres in South Korea, citing some of the above grievances. Military prostitution has always been a sensitive issue in the Koreas because of the Japanese occupation policy of comfort women. Various South Korean women claimed in the 1990s that they had been reluctant prostitutes for US forces and claimed compensation. This fuelled even more South Korean anti-American nationalism, as did American servicemen's violence against, and occasional murder of, local women. In response, Yoon Min-suk, a singer and political activist, penned a protest song called 'Fucking USA' in 2002. K-pop stars, including PSY, the singer of the international hit 'Gangnam Style', held a major anti-American concert. PSY held up a model of an American Bradley armoured vehicle and smashed it on the stage. The chorus of one of his songs was 'Kill those fucking Yankees'. Even the South Korean movie-makers got in on the act. A 2006 monster film, *The Host*, was described as anti-American. At the end of the film the chemical agent used by US forces to kill the monster was named Agent Yellow in a reference to the devastating use of Agent Orange in Vietnam. In a rare move, North Korea praised the film because of its supposed anti-American sentiments.

And yet despite all the political spats and cultural antipathies, Seoul knows that it needs US trade and military protection.

*　　*　　*

Sunshine gestures continued despite the occasional military and political crises between the two Koreas and tensions between Washington and Seoul. President Roh Moo-hyun walked across the DMZ on 2 October 2007 and later travelled for talks with Kim Jong-il in Pyongyang. They talked of preparing an international peace treaty with their international allies. But that phase of the sunshine policy was dropped in March 2010 because of yet another military crisis caused by the sinking of the ROKS *Cheonan*.

Sinking of the ROKS *Cheonan*

Commissioned in 1989, the *Cheonan* was a corvette of the southern navy. Its main mission was coastal patrol, specializing in anti-submarine operations. It was one of the ships that took part in the First Battle of Yeonpyeong (June 1999). Images of Korean conflict nearly always conjure up infantry struggles or DMZ patrols but the defence of the naval frontiers was also a constant source of inter-Korean friction. One of the naval hotspots was the disputed maritime border in the Yellow Sea. The boundary is known as the Northern Limit Line (NLL). Pyongyang claimed on 6 June 1999 that South Koreans had illegally trespassed into North Korean waters. The north sent patrol boats to guard a small fishing fleet that had crossed the NLL in an apparent counter-provocation. As the competing flotillas built up, a North Korean patrol boat collided with a South Korean vessel, causing minor damage. By 11 June the South Korean navy began what was called a 'bumping offensive' by pushing their rivals. This escalated with the north doing the same. Within days the bumping became more like ramming. Eventually a North Korean patrol boat, after being pincered between two South Korean naval ships, opened fire with its machine guns and 25mm cannon. The ROK navy responded with machine guns and cannon fire – over 4,500 rounds were expended by the southern forces. One North Korean torpedo boat was sunk and severe damage was inflicted on other northern patrol boats. Pyongyang admitted that thirty North Korean sailors had been killed but Seoul estimated that it might have been three times that number. The south's losses were relatively light – some damage to their ships and nine sailors slightly injured.

This was a victory for the south, although Pyongyang claimed a major triumph and massive damage to the rival navy. For a while the northern navy kept to its side of the NLL. Another similar minor encounter happened in 2002, known as the Second Battle of Yeonpyeong. In November 2010 the north attacked the island of Yeonpyeong itself.

This was the context for the *Cheonan* sinking. On 6 March 2010 an explosion occurred in the stern of the ship and it almost immediately broke in two. The cause of the explosion was not known then. The ship sank just off the coast of Baengnyeong island with the loss of forty-six members of its crew of a hundred and four. Eventually the major parts of the ship were salvaged. Most investigating naval experts, but not all, in South Korea and US Navy specialists concluded that a torpedo fired from a North Korean submarine was to blame. Naturally, the North Korean and Chinese naval experts disagreed. Nevertheless, Seoul said it would cut all trade with the north; the north responded by abrogating previous non-aggression agreements.

On 23 November 2010 North Korean artillery fired at Yeonpyeong island inside southern waters but only seven-and-a-half miles from the North Korean coast line. The island's defenders returned fire. On the island four were killed and a dozen wounded. Because both military and civilian personnel had been killed and injured, many of the island's small civilian population were then evacuated. Seoul threatened the destruction of a nearby North Korean missile base if the attacks were repeated.

The launch into earth orbit in December 2012 of a North Korean satellite prompted an escalation of tensions in the region, especially when Pyongyang later launched missiles overflying Japan. The fiery North Korean rhetoric also suggested an imminent nuclear attack on its enemies – this was part of the new leader, Kim Jong-un, establishing his military credentials. Four senior southern military officers were abducted and northern drones were found with onboard cameras that had captured sensitive sites including the Blue House, the president's residence. Firing of artillery rounds by the north and increased propaganda by the south were small beer compared with the massive advances in northern nuclear weapons' technology, proved by bomb tests and ICBM launches.

The South Korean leadership never gave up hope of renewed détente. President Park Geun-hye kept trying with her 'trustpolitik'. In 2014, however, she gave a speech in Dresden that Korea could emulate the German model. Pyongyang interpreted this as meaning that the south would swallow the north as West Germany had incorporated its eastern kin and so dubbed President Park a 'freakish old maid'. When Park met both President Obama and Prime Minister Shinzo Abe of Japan at a trilateral meeting in The Hague, North Korean media called Park a 'dirty prostitute' and said that the US president was her 'pimp'. Later the official North Korean news agency called Obama a 'cross-breed with unclear blood' and that he had 'the figure of a monkey'. This was not ideal vocabulary for Pyongyang to navigate its way out of its pariah status.

President Obama continued his policy of strategic patience. That did not mean inaction. As early as 2013, Seoul had asked the Pentagon about the THAAD system. The Terminal High Altitude Area Defense was designed to protect against North Korean missiles. Seoul and Washington haggled about the price and South Korea talked about alternatives such as the Israeli Arrow 3. Beijing raised concerns that the THAAD could be used offensively rather than defensively. THAAD was originally developed because of the US experience with Iraq's Scud missiles during the Gulf War of 1991. The THAAD interceptor carried no warhead but relied on the kinetic energy of impact to destroy the incoming missile. A kinetic energy hit minimizes the risk of exploding conventional-warhead missiles and the warhead of nuclear-tipped ballistic missiles will not detonate upon a kinetic-energy hit – in theory at least. The US system, largely built by Lockheed Martin, was installed in the United Arab Emirates, Israel and Romania. Eventually, in July 2016, agreement was reached to deploy the controversial system to counter the chronic threat level from North Korea. Two THAAD systems were initially installed in 2017. Each unit consisted of six truck-mounted launchers, forty-eight interceptors, a fire-control and communications unit and an AN/TPY-2 radar. This would supplement the existing Patriot systems as well as Aegis destroyers capable of stopping ballistic missiles. Seoul agreed to pay for the kit and Washington said it would fund the costs of operating the systems.

Other Washington–Seoul issues still niggled. The off-set costs – the amount South Korea should contribute towards America's extensive deployments – continued to cause friction, as did the operational control of the US and South Korean forces. Seoul always feared that if South Koreans took completely independent command, then the US commitment could weaken. In nearly all cases, the North Koreans could be relied on to be highly provocative and on time; thus the increased threat level would tend to encourage agreement between the US and South Korean allies, as in the case of THAAD. Yet, fundamentally, most South Koreans wanted to reduce the northern threat, not erect more and more expensive defence systems.

Walking on sunshine

When President Moon Jae-in was elected president of the south in May 2017 he promised to revive the sunshine policy. In response, the northern regime suggested a joint delegation to the forthcoming Winter Olympics in Seoul. North and South duly marched together at the Olympic opening ceremony and fielded a joint women's ice hockey team. The North Koreans sent a high-powered delegation, including the boss's right-hand woman, his sister, Kim Yo-jong. The South Korean media were mesmerized by the First Sister and called her the 'Ivana Trump of the DPRK'. The first lady, Ri Sol-ju, was a glamourous addition to the normally grey style of the North Korean leadership. With her at his side, Kim Jong-un looked like a modern leader while his sister worked assiduously in the background, albeit less decorously attired than her sister-in-law. The north also sent musicians to perform for their southern brothers and sisters. After the Olympics, K-pop stars were sent north, although strictly instructed to tone down any suggestive dance routines and tunes for the more puritan northerners.

On 27 April 2018 President Moon Jae-in met the northern dictator in the Joint Security Area at Panmunjom and the southern president took the first steps into the north since the DMZ was set up. They met three times that year, including a state visit to Pyongyang. The South Korean president was allowed to deliver a heartfelt speech to a receptive audience of 50,000 in Pyongyang. In the north the party theology dictated that only one charismatic leader could shine. President Moon appeared to be well-received in the north (despite his southern nickname of 'Dark King' from a Japanese manga series, *One Piece*, an ironic epithet for someone primarily associated with sunshine). The two Korean leaders talked about practical means of re-unification, not least the connection and modernization of their railways. Little steps ensued – the north adjusted its time zone to match the south. Seoul ordered the propaganda loudspeakers to be removed from the DMZ and tried to stop South Koreans flying balloons, carrying anti-regime leaflets, over the border. Family reunions were re-started. Some guard posts in the DMZ were taken down. The two sides also worked hard at restoring not just the strategic hotline but general communications, not least to prevent accidental clashes on land and sea. And so it went on – some advances were practical, such as communications; others were more symbolic, such as sending joint teams to the 2018 Asian games in Indonesia.

For sunshine not to become moonshine, as some critics dubbed it (adapting the term from the president's surname), the double act had to become a ménage a trois. It would require President Trump to meet with both men and also to form a bond with Kim Jong-un, the 'Little Rocket Man' as the US president had called him. The Donald had always prided himself on his ability to make a deal. In the beginning it looked as though the US was going to war with North Korea. But that was the Republican president's modus operandi – talk tough and then soften up his opponent for the final deal. In business, many of Trump's numerous enterprises had ended in bankruptcy. The equivalent regarding Korea was possibly nuclear war.

The sunshine policy was named after Aesop's fable about the sun and wind competing to convince a traveller to remove his coat; the liberal approach argued that a warm engagement, through trade, economic zones, tourism and cultural exchanges, would lead to a more open North Korea. The obverse, it was claimed, would lead to more sanctions and a greater risk of nuclear war. The biggest risk of the sunshine policy was that it would confirm the status quo by providing time and funds to Pyongyang. Conditions did improve, however; the mood in 2019 in both Koreas was a far cry from the apocalyptic paranoia of the late '50s and '60s or, for that matter, 2017.

The debate was still intense about whether the hawks were right: tough confrontation worked better than economic warmth. Sunshine or darkness seemed often to have little direct bearing on the Kim dynasty, concerned above all with family preservation. The notion that North Korea was about to implode was the eternal hope of Western opponents; likewise, it was long assumed that the Chinese economic miracle would lead inevitably to multi-party democracy. Western experts have been proved wrong about both. Equally, few Sovietologists predicted the rapid collapse of the USSR. So, too, the long argument about sanctions on apartheid South Africa led to numerous contradictions in Western policy. The USSR toppled itself and soon became authoritarian Russia while South Africa reformed itself and became, briefly, the rainbow nation before succumbing to regional bad habits and 'Zimbabweanization' because of its inefficiencies and corruption.

So would stick or carrot or both work better with Pyongyang? The old notion of a northern implosion and absorption by the south – the West German model – seemed highly unlikely. The North Vietnamese example became increasingly unlikely, too, as a North Korean conventional invasion threat waned. Stern critics of sunshine said that the south ignored the terrible human rights super-violations in the north. Giving so much money to the Kim dictatorship only prolonged the agony of the ordinary North Korean citizens, they said. Yet Seoul has tended to avoid the idea of conditionality – trade and aid in exchange for tangible reforms. This was just 'horse-trading' as the north called it. Instead, Seoul talked of 'flexible reciprocity' based on Confucian values. As the so-called 'older brother' in the family, the south would assist the north without expecting immediate and specific paybacks. The south would not bargain with lives by withholding humanitarian aid.

Yet southern hawks believed that the sunshine policy weakened the main pillar of South Korea's stability – the alliance with the USA. Seoul tended to privilege the north not least by glossing over its regular iniquities and not condemning their human rights abuses at the UN. Peaceful re-unification, hawks argued, could result only from strength, not least by a strong partnership with America. Should Pyongyang be fought or appeased? Neither Washington nor Seoul came up with a convincing solution.

Chapter 9

Japan – The Old Imperial Power

As the former imperial power, it is not surprising that relations between the DPRK and Japan have generally been strained. Much of the historical propaganda in North Korea has been based on fighting the Japanese before 1945 especially the heroics of the state's founder, Kim Il-sung. The antagonism has been reciprocated for various reasons, not least the question of the DPRK's abduction of Japanese citizens. In a 2014 poll by the BBC, 91 per cent of the Japanese were hostile to the DPRK. The north tried to manipulate hostilities between Seoul and Tokyo, for example over the issue of so-called 'comfort women' – perhaps 200,000 Korean girls, usually virgins under 18, were forced into prostitution for the imperial forces. (Chinese, Malay, Dutch, Philippine and many other Asian females were also made to work at 'comfort stations', or brothels.) In the late 1950s North Korea encouraged the voluntary repatriation of Koreans in Japan: hundreds of thousands had moved there, mainly for work, in the imperial period. The Koreans in Japan were by and large affiliated to two main rival organizations, *Mindan,* which favoured South Korea, and *Chosen Soren* (Japanese)/*Chochongryon* (Korean) which supported the DPRK.

Pyongyang desperately needed the expertise of trained personnel and they were more likely to come from Japan than South Korea. The DPRK made numerous and expansive promises to the members of *Chosen Soren* about the wonderful life and jobs they could have if they returned to re-build the homeland, as a prelude to an imminent re-unification. By late 1960 around 50,000 Koreans of an estimated 600,000 had been transported in Soviet ships. The programme was extended because another 60,000 wanted to be repatriated.

Initially some Japanese-Koreans did well, but many faced discrimination, as they had previously in Japan. Many were forced to sell their possessions, especially Japanese domestic goods – much cherished in the DPRK – in order to survive. As one Korean from Japan put it,

They felt that North Korea had received them not as compatriots but as foreigners – worse, as foreigners who were responsible for being so. The North Korean state was eager to collect the Japanese residents' money, but it made no effort to dispel the distrust many natives felt towards the newly arrived ...[They] couldn't officially request to return to Japan. Doing so could even be dangerous. Their unhappy decision to move to North Korea was irreversible, and they all thought of themselves as prisoners.[1]

Even the committed communists among the returnees sometimes fell foul of the regime and whole families, often three generations, were incarcerated in prison camps. Many Japanese spouses of Korean men who had returned to the DPRK were not allowed to go back or even communicate with relatives in Japan. Relations soured even more when North Korea gave asylum to elements of the Japanese Red Army, designated a terrorist organization by Tokyo. The Japanese government also grew increasingly angry at the refusal of the DPRK to pay its bills accrued via the semi-official trading channels.

As Japan became an economic superpower, Tokyo began a rapprochement with its old enemies in Beijing and Pyongyang. Japan tried to balance its trade ties with both Koreas but did not open up full diplomatic relations with Pyongyang. North Korean aims were to boost trade with Japan while discouraging Tokyo from too close a relationship with Seoul. Also North Korea, like China, was hostile to Japanese re-armament.

Eventually moves to resume diplomatic relations bore some fruit in 1991. Pyongyang wanted a formal apology and compensation for the military occupation of Korea. Tokyo removed its opposition to North Korea joining the UN at the same time as Seoul joined. The question of compensation continued to prove difficult, however. North Korea's problems caused by the collapse of the USSR forced Pyongyang to reduce its regional isolation and so there was a need for some rapprochement with Tokyo.

During the years 1977 to 1983 North Korea had abducted scores of Japanese citizens, not least to teach Japanese in espionage colleges. Some had died but Tokyo wanted the survivors returned. Many North Koreans still relied on money sent from the wise relatives who had stayed in Japan. Some critics in Tokyo wanted the remittances to be stopped, not least to put pressure on outstanding questions such as abductions, as well as general anxiety about nuclear weapons. Tokyo imposed various sanctions on the DPRK. In 2007, for example, Japan imposed a six-month ban on the ferry service and charter flights to North Korea and also tightened restrictions on export controls and bank remissions. In early 2015 Tokyo responded to continuing North Korean threats by extending sanctions that were due to expire in May. And the Japanese police raided the premises of *Chongryon* (the General Association of Korean Residents in Japan), Pyongyang's de facto representative in Tokyo, because of alleged smuggling of high-value mushrooms. Above all, the DPRK incensed Japanese opinion by firing missiles into Japanese air space. On 17 March 2017 sirens blared as Japan held its first-ever post-1945 evacuation drills after North Korean missiles tests. 'A missile appears to have been launched from North Korea. Take cover in a building or underground,' said various announcements on TV and radio. The Japanese, especially in Hokkaido, the second largest island, were given around ten minutes warning to take cover. The DPRK's Hwasong-12 missile did no physical harm, nor did it cause panic in Japan. Some of the famous never-late bullet trains and even a few golf competitions were temporarily halted, however. Nevertheless, a flurry of civil defence activities ensued, which some critics of the Japanese government alleged were used to boost its expanding arsenal.

*   *   *

Because of the umbilical security connections between Washington, Tokyo and Seoul, Japan recognized South Korea in 1965 as the sole legitimate government of the whole peninsula. But relations were not smooth, not least over disputed territorial claims (such as Liancourt Rocks) as well as Japan's foot-dragging over its apology for the military occupation, plus the question of 200,000 Korean comfort women – of whom around three-quarters died after the traumas of being raped by soldiers thirty to forty times a day. Eventually, when most of the surviving women had died, in 2008 Japan agreed to pay a lump sum and monthly payments to the remaining victims. Amid all the publicity about the comfort women survivors, the Seoul government went a long way to make their retirement as comfortable as possible. The *'halmoni'* (an affectionate term for grandmothers) were often offered comfortable accommodation in a 'house of sharing' as the homes were called. Some of the grandmothers, however, claimed that the Seoul government had sold them short on deals with Tokyo, and lodged a private law suit. Japan made a final settlement in December 2015.

More recent Tokyo–Seoul disputes have centred on fish imports from Japan that Seoul claimed were polluted by the Fukushima nuclear meltdown. The Japanese responded by sanctioning key hi-tech items from going to South Korea. Japan stopped three chemicals that were crucial to South Korea's semi-conductor industry. The export-driven South Korean economy, led by big technology groups such as Samsung, SK Hynix and LG Electronics, rely heavily on materials from Japan. In addition, legal disputes over claims by individual Korean citizens against Japanese forced labour went on until 2019. Despite these disagreements Korean culture became fashionable in Japan, especially K-pop. The so-called 'Korean wave' inspired a fad for Korean movies and TV series.

Washington co-operated closely on security and intelligence matters with both Tokyo and Seoul, not just because of the North Korean threat but also because of Chinese maritime expansion. Nevertheless, Seoul has shown some concern about Japan using the North Korean bellicosity as an excuse for its own military growth. Various military incidents, for example over a South Korean destroyer locking on to a Japanese maritime patrol aircraft with missile-targeting radar, have increased tensions. In late 2019 both countries fell out over bilateral intelligence-sharing protocols. Japan has traditionally placed more importance on intelligence gathered from the US although it will probably become more cumbersome for Japan to secure information from Seoul regarding North Korean defectors. In the final analysis Tokyo will continue to align itself closely with Washington, not least on dealing with the 'Little Rocket Man'.

Japan has been the most enthusiastic participant in the American missile defence plans in the region, deploying long-range AN/TPY-2 X-band radars, ship-based Aegis tracking systems equipped with SM-3 interceptors, and ground-to-air PAC-3 interceptor missiles. It was also planning to install a land-based version of Aegis instead of THAAD.

China has always feared a mini-NATO on its own doorstep. South Korea, however, has always avoided over-close ties with Tokyo – even on BMD (Ballistic Missile Defence) – because of its historical aversion to military co-operation with Japan. Also, Seoul feared irritating China. South Korea's attitude towards America has sometimes been ambivalent. Yet, according to a 2017 Pew survey, 57 per cent of people in Japan had a favourable view of the United States while 75 per cent had a favourable view of the American people. A 2018 Gallup poll showed that 87 per cent of Americans had a favourable view of Japan.

The US has traditionally stationed around 50,000 soldiers and 10,000 Marines in America's large bases in Japan, especially Okinawa. Despite trade disputes, Japan has been a towering pillar of US strategic power in Asia, to protect South Korea, Taiwan as well as the Philippines against constant Chinese encroachment in the South China Sea and general threats from Pyongyang.

Chapter 10

The Big Brother – China

In the strictly Confucian way of thinking, the People's Republic of China had been North Korea's big brother who had protected the tiny neighbour. They shared a unique mutual aid and co-operation treaty that promised military support if the other were attacked by an outside power. The treaty was renewed twice and it is valid until 2021. Beijing was for long relatively friendly with Pyongyang but the new economic superpower had grown increasingly exasperated with the way that North Korea's rhetoric and nuclear programme threatened not only regional war but also economic instability. Washington tried to make China the main enforcer of Kim Jong-un's behaviour. Beijing's public response was to call for peaceful resolutions of the nuclear dispute and argued that the best way was for direct negotiations between the American superpower and the minuscule rogue state. Until 2018 the trend was downhill in their relationship but it improved thereafter partly because of concern at any possibility of serious détente in North Korean-US relations. Beijing wanted the US and Pyongyang to talk but not to get too cosy. Beijing was always concerned with both regional economic and political stability.

Ever since the Korean War Pyongyang had appeared to take Beijing's support somewhat for granted. To a certain extent, that is. The so-called August Faction Incident in 1956 was the shorthand for Chinese and Russian projected intervention to change the North Korean leadership. In the 1960s the Korean Workers' Party criticized the upheaval of the Cultural Revolution and described Mao as 'an old fool who has gone out of his mind'. Beijing recalled its ambassador in October 1966 and complained of North Korean 'revisionism', a heavy-duty insult in the communist lexicon.

When Kim Jong-il died in December 2011, Beijing worried about an implosion during the succession. In the previous year Wikileaks indicated that US state department messages suggested that senior figures in

Beijing had regarded their supposed North Korean ally as a 'spoiled child'. The leaked diplomatic traffic indicated that both Washington and Seoul were discussing the Chinese intimations that they would prefer re-unification under Seoul rather than the maverick regime in Pyongyang. Chinese officials assessed that they could have coped with an influx of perhaps 300,000 North Korean refugees following a collapse in Pyongyang. Beijing thought that the Chinese military might have to be deployed to seal the border. The PLA would not be used *inside* North Korea, however. The younger cadres in the Chinese Communist Party did not regard the North Koreans as useful allies and they did not want to risk another war. The leaked diplomatic cables indicated that if re-unification came under Seoul then Beijing would not welcome a US military presence north of the DMZ. China did not want a unified Korea that was hostile to its interests.[1]

North Korea did not implode but Beijing watched the behaviour of the new inexperienced leader with some concern. In December 2013 Kim Jong-un's uncle, Jang Song-thaek, was executed for treason. The uncle, a favourite intermediary with the Chinese, was rumoured to have wanted to reform North Korea along the economic lines of Beijing's domestic programme. This was interpreted by Kim Jong-un as an attempt to replace him with a Beijing favourite. Others in the North Korean party were arrested, killed and punished for alleged pro-Chinese reformism. Of course 'reform' was a word that implied faults that had to be remedied. For so long the hermit kingdom's leadership could only insist that their system was perfect.

In the spring of 2014 the Beijing-controlled *Global Times* ran an editorial complaining, in unusually harsh language, about 'the international isolation, poverty and risks of anger' if the DPRK conducted another nuclear test. China had recently castigated North Korea for not giving advance notice of a rocket test that came within minutes of hitting a Chinese passenger jet. By 2015 the Chinese trade with South Korea was thirty times greater than with Pyongyang. China had become South Korea's largest trading partner by far and the biggest source of foreign investment. Inevitably the massive economic ties with Beijing were bound to influence Seoul's security ties with China. And China had to weigh up the imbalance between the north and south in economic ties versus Beijing's traditional military ties with its rogue neighbour. China has long maintained a policy of working with pariah states in its search for minerals and oil. Sudan, Myanmar and the Democratic Republic of Congo were obvious examples. But these weren't next-door neighbours. Chinese businessmen complain all the time about the hazards of doing business in North Korea. At the same time the DPRK fears an eventual economic or even political absorption by China which has ancient territorial claims on North Korea.

Although trade matters and later a (very) limited sanctions policy imposed by Beijing undermined relations, as did the impounding by Pyongyang of Chinese fishing boats, the real bone of contention is the nuclear programme and especially North Korea's threat to launch missiles on continental USA. Beijing is also worried about nuclear testing near the Chinese border. The northern neighbour also has serious safety concerns about the DPRK'S reactors: it does not want another Chernobyl on its doorstep. Beijing started imposing sanctions in 2016. When China stopped importing coal in February 2017, Pyongyang accused its big benefactor of dancing to the tune of American imperialists. Nonetheless, Kim Jong-un was hosted graciously by the General Secretary, Xi Jinping, in Beijing in March 2018.

Chinese support was crucial to Pyongyang; it is by far North Korea's largest trading partner. China provides about half of North Korean imports. The coal embargo in 2017 hit the north hard as coal was North Korea's main export. Beijing was showing its displeasure at the continued nuclear tests, and also partly because of world pressure.

An assassination too far

It was an unremarkable Monday morning in February 2017 at Kuala Lumpur International Airport. At a check-in kiosk, a Korean business traveller was waiting for attention. A pretty young woman was seen trying to get Kim 'John' Chol's attention. Suddenly the chubby middle-aged man felt the sensation of something wet and cold on his face. As he recoiled in surprise, another woman, wearing a black glove and a white T-shirt with LOL on the front, grabbed his head from behind and started smearing an oily substance over his mouth and cheeks. Then both assailants rushed away in opposite directions and melted into the crowds.

In shock, Kim's heart started to pound rapidly as he stumbled towards the lavatories but then changed his mind; he staggered towards a group of security officials. Security TV cameras filmed a group of well-dressed and seated Asian men intently watching Kim's death throes. By the time Kim had been helped to the airport's clinic, his vision was blurred and his nervous system was beginning to shut down. On his way to hospital he suffered a series of convulsions before a final fatal seizure. It was claimed that he was killed by VX nerve gas applied in two separate liquid applications, combining into a fatal mixture, so as to allow the two duped assassins a chance of survival.

Kim Jong-nam was not with any of the bodyguards he used to travel with. He had written recently to his half-brother, the great dictator in Pyongyang, and assumed that, with his Chinese protection, he would be OK. But blood feuds are all part of the ruling dynasty's game of thrones.

Beijing was angry with its difficult neighbour. The Chinese did not accept that Kim Jong-nam was a CIA agent or double agent. There was some evidence, however, that Kim met with US agents in Singapore and Malaysia. From his base in Macau, Kim was apparently laundering the 100-dollar US bills that Pyongyang was mass producing. These fake 'Benjamins' were called superdollars because the forgeries were so good. Whatever he was up to, it was generally understood that Kim was under the protection of Beijing, whether he was considered an actual substitute for his half-brother or not. More Chinese pressure was now put on Kim Jong-un.

*   *   *

Later, however, Beijing eased off on some of the economic pressures. It is said to want to avoid the regime collapse causing a seismic wave of refugees across the 870-mile border. The Trump-led detente between North Korea and the USA appeared to have paved the way for Pyongyang's balancing rapprochement with China's Xi Jinping. Still, friction persisted. In November 2017 China called on North Korea to cease increasing tensions by missile launches. Yet Beijing had been very lukewarm and evasive about recent sanctions. Beijing had not hesitated to show that it could be a big brother who could wield a big stick. In

2018 Chinese imports from North Korea plummeted by 88 per cent and exports were reduced by 33 per cent. The *informal* trade along the border increased however – ranging from fuel, seafood and cell phones. Yet the physical and transport links had been improved as well by the construction of economic zones close by the border on both sides.

China – along with Japan, South Korea and the USA – had provided probably around 75 per cent of the food aid since 1995. The North Korean famine in the 1990s killed up to 2.4 million people. Poor management, droughts and severe flooding all made things worse. The UN estimated that up to 43 per cent of the population were malnourished.

While the Chinese government would prefer their truculent dependency not to have nuclear weapons, the greatest fear used to be collapse. The spectre of hundreds of thousands fleeing north worried Beijing. Yet one thing would be worse for the Chinese – a renewed war on the peninsula, especially one involving a nuclear exchange with the USA. Beijing has intimated that if Pyongyang initiates conflict with America, the Chinese government would not honour its treaty obligation and instead remain neutral. Some intelligence experts suggested that Chinese troops would not become involved in defending the Kim family despotism and instead deploy its strength to forge a new regime more to its own liking. Nevertheless, at the time of writing, the Chinese supreme leader and the North Korean supremo had met four times à deux.

North Korea survived only because of massive Chinese support, despite the later equivocation. Yet the USA counted far more with Beijing than the often bloodyminded dictator in Pyongyang. Washington wanted North Korea to give up its nukes in return for trade, aid, diplomatic benefits and normalization of relations. The on-off love affair between the Chinese leader and Donald Trump confounded many experts but the American drive to reduce the large bilateral trade deficit made some sense. It was Donald Trump's cowboy style that concerned so many diplomats. According to Victor Cha of the Center for Strategic and International Studies, Trump's approach was two-fold: 'The first phase was to treat China as part of the solution and, if that didn't work, then treat them as part of the problem.'

China consistently tried to avoid war, and to ensure stability. Beijing demanded an influential role in any solution if North Korea were to implode or if it didn't and even re-united with the south. As ever, China looked after its own national interests. And its status – and geography – should guarantee that Beijing is prominent in any deals regarding de-nuclearization or indeed re-unification of the two Koreas.

Beijing had also tried to improve ties with Seoul. Xi Jinping had met a number of recent South Korean presidents; China was South Korea's top trading partner in 2018. Beijing was trying to deploy leverage with the south and with the West. Xi thought little of his Comrade Neighbour right from the start. They had not met at all in the first five years both were in supreme power. Once Beijing-Pyongyang relations had been described as 'close as lips and teeth'. Not only was Kim Jong-un perceived to be regularly winding up the Americans, he also seemed to be doing the same to his remaining friends in Beijing. The North Koreans launched three missiles on the very day that Xi was hosting leaders of the twenty largest economies in the Chinese city of Hangzhou. Another salvo the following year detracted from Xi's opening of an international forum for his cherished Belt and Road project. Both Xi and Trump were much closer to each other than either was to the Little Rocket Man. When Trump suddenly changed direction and started talking to his old enemy, China was caught unawares and had to recalibrate relations with its rogue neighbour.

So, for the first time since 2005, when Hu Jintao visited, a Chinese supremo decided to fly into Pyongyang. Tong Zhao, a fellow at the Carnegie-Tsinghua Centre for Global Policy, explained: the main aim of Xi's visit was to re-affirm ties, amid the deepening Washington-Beijing trade war, and to show that China's role in a settlement of North Korea could not be ignored. Tong Zhao said:

> As China-US strategic rivalry grows, China wants to maintain its geopolitical influence on the Korean peninsula. By demonstrating its unique relations with the DPRK at a time when neither Washington nor Seoul is able to resume high-level engagements with Pyongyang, Beijing is signalling to Washington that it is still a helpful, constructive and indispensable partner to resolve important regional problems.

The strategic context

China's economic and military growth has been so striking that it has often caused kneejerk reactions in the US and Europe. Put simply, two main schools of thought exist in the West:

- The peaceful China. Its new strategic cosmopolitanism is geared to expanding its national interest – not ideology – primarily to secure energy sources and to improve its trading patterns with the EU and US.
- The difficult China. China's outreach is part of an exclusionary policy with illiberal and rogue states. North Korea has been the prime example. It develops trade patterns that ignore all human rights concerns. This undermines Western conditionality strategies that aim to improve conditions in autocratic countries, not least in Africa. China could manipulate its vast US dollar surpluses to bring down the American economy, though that would not be in Beijing's immediate interest, particularly when it's stealing Western intellectual property worth tens of billions of dollars, especially by cyber raids.

Chinese foreign policy has been sufficiently nuanced – proverbially 'inscrutable' – to allow a variety of interpretations. Washington's policies toward Beijing contained elements of mutual economic co-operation but also strategies, especially with Japan, that could have been perceived by the Chinese as military threats. The problem is mutual threat perceptions work both ways, just as Kaiser Bill's Germany felt 'encircled' while its neighbours felt menaced, or Moscow believed that NATO was encroaching into its sphere of influence. If a dispassionate observer looked at the numerous US bases that surround China, you can see why the country – historically a land power – started building a bigger navy.

China has a massive population problem. The 90 per cent Han inhabitants were crammed into the plains of the heartlands. They looked West as the Americans did. Just as the Iron Horse brought white settlers to the lands of the Apache and Navajo and other great Native American tribes, so the new Chinese railways have been bringing the Han to Tibet, for example. Now there is much to be said for Richard Gere and his fellow activists: the Himalayan cultures of Tibet, especially, but also Nepal and Bhutan deserve great respect. But any real understanding of China must be contextualized by its long history of war partly caused by the main invasion routes, from the Mongols to the century of humiliation when Western powers dominated the country and then the Japanese raped and pillaged. And the Americans threw their weight around in the civil war between the nationalists and the communists. The Chinese have just concerns about securing their borders.

To continue with the American historical analogy, the geopolitical writer Robert Kaplan expounded the theory that the South China Sea is to the Chinese today what the Caribbean was to the USA at the beginning of the twentieth century. The Americans, after they had consolidated their land mass by conquering the Wild West, had become a two-ocean power (Atlantic and Pacific) and then moved to control the seas around them, pushing the Spanish out of Cuba, for example, and then endlessly meddling in much weaker South American countries. Both the USA and China feel themselves exceptional states – America's 'manifest destiny' and China's variations on the 'mandate of heaven'. One of the few Americans who fully understands China and is respected by their leaders is Henry Kissinger. In his magisterial *On China* Kissinger makes a number of important points. He says, 'The world order, as concurrently instituted, was built largely without Chinese participation. Hence China feels less bound by rules in the creation of which it did not participate.' He has also emphasized the fear that China has of outside powers threatening its periphery and therefore posing a threat to its heartland and its domestic institutions. When China did perceive such threats it went to war – in Korea in 1950, against India in 1962, along the northern border with the USSR in 1969 and against Vietnam ten years later. Some of these threats were very real, not least from the American generals of the time. Some of them wanted to use nukes when Chinese armies overwhelmed the US-led coalition in Korea. It was arguably a close-run affair: America could have used nukes in anger a second time, and only just a few years after the atomic bombing of Japan.

At the time of the Korean War the communist leadership in Beijing was only one year on from the end of the long civil war with the American-backed nationalists. Today the communist party is in the ascendancy both at home and abroad. After taking over as general secretary of the Chinese Communist Party in November 2012, Xi Jinping has secured his dominance very rapidly and has also flaunted his dominance, though not cultivating a personality cult like Mao's. President Xi has dumped the collective leadership and his grip has been strengthened by an intensive nationwide anti-corruption campaign that appears genuinely popular with the masses. China was always diffident about accepting the mantle of great power; not any more, not least in relation to the USA. The massive economic surge has dropped to 6–7 per cent; that is still humbling for the Western growth rate, especially in the EU. In 1981 the Chinese economy accounted for less than 3 per cent of the world output; in 2019 it was perhaps about 20 per cent.

Both Obama's so-called 'pivot' towards Asia and Trump's plan for a 350-ship navy were designed to check China, especially as it is seen by Washington and its Asian allies as a threat, not least in the South China Sea. The Chinese were mightily offended by Trump's early conversation with the Taiwanese president and the suggestion that the US would go back to the two Chinas policy. (There are of course *four* Chinas besides the mainland and Taiwan – namely, Hong King and Singapore. But that is another story.) The US has armed Taiwan to the teeth and would probably go to war to defend it – unless Taiwan declares independence. This would destroy Beijing's myth of One China, and probably prompt a reciprocal declaration of war by Beijing. The whole US-Beijing-Taipei diplomatic triangle has been based on a hypocritical myth. But it has been a convenient myth that, so far, has prevented war. Trump's provocative attitudes regarding Taiwan as well as the withdrawal from the Trans-Pacific Partnership trade deal disturbed the region. Part of President Xi's new assertiveness was his personal assumption of the position of military commander in chief after a shake-up of the general staff. He has given himself operational control of the Chinese nuclear trigger. The Chinese president has also congratulated himself on the unveiling of the country's first homemade aircraft carrier as opposed to a pimped-up ex-Soviet rust-bucket. China was still way behind the US Navy but its advanced ground-based missile systems could play havoc with an American fleet that came too close to the mainland and China's fighter aircraft are capable and plentiful.

Trump made a diplomatic gaffe when he launched his first act of war (by attacking Syria) when President and Mrs Xi Jinping were visiting the so-called summer White House in Florida in April 2017. The Chinese leader had hidden it but he must have felt affronted by being involved – no matter how accidently – in such a dramatic assault not just on President Assad but also on Russian prestige. It was also a dent to Chinese pride, unless Trump took the very unlikely precaution of *fully* briefing the boss of the Chinese Communist Party. American diplomats tried to spin the probable insult to the Chinese president by suggesting that he was privately rather impressed by Trump's macho stance. Unlikely. They talked trade but many potential powder kegs surround the two presidents, besides North Korea.

Accidental conflict in the South China Sea has equally been a trigger to real fighting talk. The Pentagon sent a number of planes to fly in what China claimed was restricted air space. And soon after Trump took over as president, an aircraft carrier strike group, led by the USS *Carl Vinson*, was sent to the South China Sea to demonstrate that its sea lanes were open to international trade. Trump's literary claim to fame was his book *The Art of the Deal,* which was entirely ghosted. The Chinese general Sun Tzu wrote the much better *Art of War* more than two and a half millennia before. It would be foolish to underestimate the Chinese.

The most important strategic question of the beginning of the twenty-first century was whether the USA could peacefully accommodate the rise and rise of China. To Trump, it was a matter of business transactions. For him, the $375-billion US trade deficit with Beijing was prime evidence that China was cheating and taking advantage of previous administrations who were too soft. Trump said he would stand up to the Chinese; he was also surrounded by foreign policy hawks. Vice President Mike Pence had been a long-time critic of China's very poor human rights record. For example, the pogroms of China's Muslims, the Uighurs, became a hot question in 2018 and Hong Kong's freedoms came to prominence in mid-2019. John Bolton, the national security adviser (until mid-2019), as well as Mike Pompeo, the secretary of state, were all longstanding hawks on China. These critics attacked the old shibboleth that economic growth inevitably would produce more representative government. Instead China had become more Orwellian, and President Xi had made himself

Big Brother for life, even though the Chinese economy had, arguably, overtaken America's.

Trump had dealt with China with a characteristic mix of personal affability and tweeted threats. That had been his single consistency in a foreign policy that normally careened off in different directions – from casual sabre-rattling to slavish embrace of dictators, but always the regular threats of tariff wars. Vice President Pence seemed to have been given the role of bad cop regarding China. He ranged from his original theme of abysmal human rights to the economic threat (notably the Belt and Road initiative) as well as the menace of Chinese naval expansion in the South China Sea. Nevertheless, Pence was careful to avoid parroting the hackneyed lexicon of the Cold War.

The USSR was proverbially 'Upper Volta with rockets'. The People's Republic completely dwarfed the USSR in economic prowess. China and America had become economically integrated in a way that would have been unimaginable between the two almost sealed spheres of influence in the Soviet and US-led blocs. China became America's biggest creditor, hoarding tens of billions of dollars in US Treasury bonds. In the original Cold War the potential battlefields were clearly delineated in Europe (though in the Third World the battle-lines were more amorphous). China appeared to be expanding across all sort of old frontiers – especially in cyberspace. Trump wanted to challenge an economy that had been founded on intellectual property theft, illegal technology transfers, currency manipulation and rabid discrimination against foreign investors. This was symbolized by Trump's pressure to keep out Huawei technology from the US and its allies. Tariffs may help, Trump argued, to bring home US companies from China and elsewhere, because the cost of goods and production in Asia would inevitably increase, thus making the domestic production, and jobs, more feasible. Trump has also tried to maintain Obama's pivot to Asia but without saying so.

Washington has tried to bolster military alliances with traditional allies such as South Korea, Japan and the Philippines as counterweights to Chinese expansionism. But Trump's aggressive stance on trade, not least with Japan, has complicated these alliances. The Donald, however, was the first US president to step on board a Japanese warship – technically 'defence-ship'. Japan does not officially have armed forces; its post-war constitution drawn up by the US does not permit a traditional military. Nevertheless, the Self-Defense Forces were slowly morphing into a real fighting force, not least because of perceived threats from China and North Korea. The helicopter carrier the JS *Kaga* was being upgraded to a traditional aircraft carrier capable of transporting some of the 105 new F-35 fighters ordered from the USA.[2] Trump was accompanied on board by the Japanese premier, Shinzo Abe. Of course, the US president did not miss the chance to praise the prime minister and the 'wonderful' US-Japanese naval relations. Meanwhile, the US still has 50,000 troops based in Japan.

Trump has also financed a rebuilding of the US navy. Military writers talk about possible US conflict with China in a way that was unthinkable a decade before. This sort of pressure is redolent of the Cold War when military competition played a major role in checkmating and finally toppling the Soviet threat. That, however, was as much an ideological collapse as an economic one. Beijing has largely ditched its Maoist ideology and adopted a very successful form of authoritarian capitalism.

No one in Washington wants war with China, nor is it considered likely but the Trumpian approach has been modelled on a Reaganesque peace through strength. Trump wants better and fairer trade relations with China and a reduction of the on-off Chinese support to North Korea. Trump prides himself on his interpersonal skills – he wants to stabilize US relations with China and North Korea.

Beijing is also trying to stabilize its sphere of influence – it is largely looking for *economic* dominance. Despite its military expansion, its military strength – especially naval – is much smaller than its American counterparts. Beijing, therefore, is being utterly pragmatic in mending its fences with its nuke-toting neighbour. Chinese foreign policy experts have been blindsided by Donald Trump's sudden cordiality with the formerly despised Little Rocket Man. Instead of fire and fury, Trump and Kim seemed to be embroiled in a bromance. Nobody in the White House knew what Trump would do next, so Beijing's confusion was understandable. The Chinese turned to their old friend Henry Kissinger to translate for them. What was Trump up to?

Chapter 11

Enter Trump

Presidential precedent

A merican presidents have long been distracted by North Korean behaviour. Obviously the big shooting war in 1950–53 absorbed much time in the White House. In 1992 Bill Clinton was invited to the country; as his presidency waned, however, he focused instead on trying to resolve the Palestine/Israel impasse. And he almost did it with the Oslo accords. It was, however, the DPRK nuclearization and then the missile capability that really started to concentrate minds in Washington.

President Bush Junior ratcheted up the tensions when he included North Korea in the axis of evil in his 2002 State of the Union address. Uranium enrichment for the weapons programme violated Pyongyang's obligations as a (then) member of the Non-Proliferation Treaty as well as the 1992 North-South Denuclearization Agreement, plus the 1994 Agreed Framework. (North Korea had been a member of the NPT from 1985 until it left in early 2003.) Again, Washington reiterated its policy that if the nuclear weapons programme was verifiably eliminated, the USA would forge a new and positive relationship with North Korea.

Ever since the Korean War, Pyongyang has always concentrated on the USA as its prime enemy and focus of threat. Under Chinese pressure, Washington went along with the six-party talks in April 2003 – the USA, China, both Koreas, Japan and Russia would try to end the long crisis.

The tempo of US-Pyongyang relations nearly always depended upon the advance of North Korea's nuclear weapons programme and the associated technology. But they also squabbled over the extent of US aid and the removal of North Korea from the US list of state sponsors of terrorism. It was the nuclear tests after 2006 that really cranked up the threat of war between America and North Korea. Should America act before Pyongyang actually acquired weapons – just as Washington felt inclined to pounce pre-emptively to dethrone Saddam Hussein?

In January 2016 North Korea conducted a fourth nuclear test and also announced that their scientists had miniaturized their nukes. The next month President Barack Obama enacted the North Korea Sanctions and Policy Enhancement Act of 2016. This passed both the Senate and the House of Representatives with hardly any dissent. Beijing warned that the sanctions could cripple North Korea's fragile economy – which was presumably the intention. Obama's failure to improve relations with the North Korean dictatorship was part of his successor's desire to do the big deal. Donald Trump often set policy as almost a kneejerk antithesis to anything that Obama had done or failed to do. This was true of North Korea as well as Iran, let alone domestic matters such as health care.

High-level visits by senior US diplomats to Pyongyang were not unknown over the years but other influential Americans made their way to the hermit kingdom. Even during the extra froideur of the Kim Il-sung period, Christian evangelist Billy Graham travelled twice to Pyongyang in search of peace. The famous evangelist met Kim Il-sung who had talked about the possibility of a 'grand bargain' with the USA. Graham was perhaps one of the first and most significant non-communist figures to visit the country, in 1992, as part of the thaw after the end of the Cold War in Europe. Graham's visit later helped pave the way for a humanitarian trip by a former president, Jimmy Carter. It also set a precedent for less pious leaders such as the hard-living basketball star, Dennis Rodman, who struck up a bromance with Kim Jong-un. Whoever they were, Washington's diplomatic and intelligence services nearly always co-ordinated closely with those who were about to be allowed into the hallowed precincts of inner Pyongyang in order to get some insight into the hermetically sealed and dangerous leadership.

The North Korean capital had once been dubbed the 'Jerusalem of the East' because of the growth of Christian missionaries before the Second World War. Graham's wife, Ruth, was born to Christian medical missionaries in China and then spent three years in Pyongyang in the 1930s. Despite her husband being one of the world's most famous Baptists, Ruth Graham remained a Presbyterian (the same Christian branch as Kim Il-sung's parents). She was an independent woman and a poet, author and theologian in her own right. Her early years in China and Korea were influential in shaping her husband's later involvement.

After the collapse of the Soviet Union, Billy Graham's visit seemed to herald the hope of a fresh relationship. The pastor had spoken to President George H.W. Bush before the trip and conveyed an oral personal message to the North Korean founder. The meetings went well and, as he left, Graham said to a *Newsweek* reporter: 'They've lost the support of the Soviet Union. I got the impression they're reaching out towards the other nations for some friends.'

Like all good communist dictatorships, Pyongyang is often brilliant in encouraging optimism in well-meaning foreigners, especially gullible Americans. Deep inside the regime's propaganda departments there must have been a special section for creating glimmers of cautious optimism. Over the decades no matter what the regime did – especially to its own people – American diplomats were always trying to find some glimmers of reform. Ruth Graham visited again without her husband in 1997 and their son, Franklin, continued the family tradition. Little evidence of the improvement in the condition of Christians emerged, however. Sometimes visiting Americans were arrested and jailed for the crime of being alleged (or real) Christian missionaries. A North Korean who escaped the country in 1992 had scathing words for the Graham family on religion under the Kim regime. The defector said: 'I want to write a letter to Billy Graham. If you want to know religion in North Korea, go to a prison camp.' In the country of Big Brother, three Kims were revered as gods – any other faith was considered dangerous apostasy.

Donald Trump

The Great Negotiator would soon meet the Great Successor although Trump is not a president to be inspired (or troubled) by any religious scruples. To say that Trump is different is a great understatement. Some of the most readable and incisive accounts of the Trumpian White House are to be found in two books (*Fire and Fury* and *Siege*) by the fly-on the wall author Michael Wolff. He wrote:

> To have worked anywhere near him [Trump] is to be confronted with the most extreme and disorienting behaviour possible …. Not only is Trump not like other presidents, he is not like anyone most

of us have ever known. Hence, everyone who has been close to him feels compelled to try to explain him and to dine out on his head-smacking peculiarities.

Trump's surviving foreign policy advisers tried hard to engage with – and educate him on – the nuances of Washington's long diplomatic fandango with North Korea's leadership. They assumed that probably Trump could not find Korea on the map. He would not listen to, or even read, the shortest briefs; the billionaire businessman relied on his intuition. Trump's key advisers, Secretary of State Pompeo and, for a while, National Security Adviser John Bolton, reduced the big box binders to one-page briefs. But Trump would not, could not, focus on just one page. 'Don't box me in,' he told his advisers. As Steve Bannon, once Trump's alt-right mentor, put it, 'He's got command presence. He *looks* the part.' The showman was in charge, a strong man making peace.

Initially, Trump called Kim Jong-un 'a total nut job' while even the revered Republican Senator John McCain called Kim 'a crazy fat kid'. McCain, though, probably knew much better. All the US intelligence analyses described Kim as a rational actor, fixated on family/regime survival.

Many outside observers looked at Trump and Kim and did not doubt who was the more rational actor. Other Western experts hoped that Trump perhaps was emulating Nixon's madman theory of politics. Nixon – like perhaps Trump – might have been volatile enough to press the red button. At least the North Vietnamese and probably the Chinese thought that. After the missile launch in July 2017 Trump said he would rain down on North Korea 'fire and fury like the world had never seen'. Trump later talked of the American military being 'locked and loaded'. At the UN General Assembly Trump said he would totally destroy North Korea if necessary. Though this had effectively long been US policy only Donald Trump could have been so blunt.

The American president also said: 'The Little Rocket Man is on a suicide mission for himself.'

Kim shot back: 'I will surely and definitely tame the mentally deranged dotard with fire.'

This is almost the braggadocio of the schoolyard but this is real because the rival alpha males are armed with nukes. And Trump, of course, claimed the much bigger nukes. Kim retaliated by threatening a limited strike on the US territory of Guam in the Pacific, including Andersen Air Force Base.

In September 2017 the USAF flew B-IB bombers from Guam, along with F-15 Eagle fighter escorts from Okinawa, Japan, to waters east of North Korea. Other operations followed that carried out mock missile launches. Japanese and South Korean aircraft were also involved. On 20 November 2017, Trump officially re-listed North Korea as a state sponsor of terrorism. All this could have led to a real war – by accident or intent. Some of the Trump language was a little like that used against Saddam before the American invasion. Both US and South Korean military intelligence had worked on possible decapitation strikes to remove Kim Jong-un. No wonder he constantly changed his itinerary at the last minute. In Japan they practised drills for incoming ordnance for the first time since 1945.

Many Western military experts supposed that Washington would opt for a 'bloody nose' strategy – a limited US airstrike on a North Korean nuclear or missile site to make the Little Rocket Man pause. The regime did not assume that Trump was bluffing. North Korean diplomats around the world started politely asking Western experts how they should translate the president's rhetoric and his tweets. They asked specifically whether Trump had sole authority to push the nuclear button.

With far more resources and access, the Chinese also reached out for reliable translators of Trump's volatility. Beijing was obviously concerned that Trump's fiery fixation with North Korea could turn into a shooting war. They also realized that as Trump had also reached out for good ties with the Chinese leader then it gave Beijing some extra leverage because of its influence – sometimes – over the headstrong Kim Jong-un. The Chinese used Henry Kissinger as a key intermediary. Although not religious, Kissinger was considered by some in the Jewish community (as well as the foreign policy network) to be a patriarch. It could be argued that the modern world was created inter alia by Jesus, Marx, Freud, Trotsky, Einstein and Kissinger – all of Jewish heritage. Trump's son-in-law is Jared Kushner, an orthodox Jew who married Ivanka

Trump who had converted to Judaism. Kushner was more concerned to implement his father-in-law's wish to achieve the really big deal – a settlement of the Palestinian imbroglio. Despite a total lack of foreign policy experience, Kushner carved out a niche for himself as the brains behind the Trumpian international policy, though 'policy' might make intuition and whim sound more authoritative than they should. The president trusted his family members; he often privately declared that he would make Kushner his secretary of state. Kissinger wisely told the son-in-law to wait – secure a major foreign policy success first, he was told by the guru. A settlement in North Korea might have to be the precursor for a final deal in Jerusalem. Other insiders in the White House sarcastically, and *sotto voce*, said that Kushner was a 'latter-day Metternich'; Kushner preferred a comparison with Kissinger. Kushner hero-worshipped the former secretary of state and constantly dropped Kissinger's name into conversations. It got so bad that Ivanka started to tease her husband by referring to 'Jared's Uncle Henry'. And a handful of businessmen with investment interests in China also joined in the backroom gambits. They and Kushner suggested to Trump that he should take a new approach with North Korea – do the deal that no one – not even Obama – had managed. And it would mean a Nobel Peace Prize too, one earned though, not just gratuitously conferred as on the first African-American president. The possibility of Trump winning the Nobel Peace Prize was encouraged by Kushner.

Nevertheless, as 2017 began to turn into 2018, war looked likely between two leaders considered mad and bad around the world, East and West. The day before the 72nd anniversary of the dropping of the atomic bomb on Nagasaki, Trump had issued his fire and fury speech. Was this a coincidence as Trump had not been known for his sense of history? His words, however, curiously echoed those of President Harry Truman after the first atomic bomb was dropped on Japan. 'It is harnessing of the basic power of the universe. Behind this air attack will follow sea and land forces in such numbers and power as they have not yet seen.'

Nobody had yet repeated the American use of nukes in combat. Was that about to change? White House defenders explained that Trump had merely been in a bad mood when he issued the apocalyptic warning during a photo op at the Trump National Golf Club. The president liked to promote his own brand when he was also threatening world war.

More sober foreign policy experts in Washington wondered whether Trump was deliberately playing chicken with Kim and consciously using the same kind of hyperbolic and bellicose rhetoric. Or was this a cynical deployment of the madman theory of politics to compel North Korea to back down – assuming Kim was more rational than Trump? The problem with even the rhetorical use of such language and red lines was that Washington might have to actually call out Kim's bluff or even – in fear or caution – react pre-emptively. The mercurial Trump might have persuaded himself that military action was needed – though his main campaign thrust was bringing US troops *home*, not swapping new Asian wars for old Middle Eastern ones. Starting another Asian war made no sense. Both Trump and the pariah in Pyongyang might have been peacocking with their military prowess in order to look tough, both at home and abroad. So was this all theatre?

In early April 2017 Trump began to warn China as well. 'If China is not going to solve North Korea, we will.' Days after that threat Trump gave the go-ahead for the US military to drop a MOAB (Mother of All Bombs) on Islamic State tunnel networks in Afghanistan. This was also designed to show Beijing and Pyongyang that Trump meant business. The growing influence of former generals in the White House (H.R. McMaster and John F. Kelly) was said to explain the increasingly bellicose rhetoric – despite the counter-intuitive maxim that the military generally tend *not* to look for military solutions to primarily political problems. Maybe Trump was trying to tell China that, despite its growing wealth and power, it did not necessarily have a final say in what happened in even its own sphere of influence. Trump still led the most powerful military of all time.

China did vote at the UN for increased sanctions on North Korea in August 2017. Trump kept up the military rhetoric – perhaps, explained some experts, to stop Beijing backsliding on sanctions as it had done on previous occasions. Such rationalizations in Washington about Trump were probably wide of the mark – the Donald was simply applying his regular bullying business methods: go in hard, then launch a charm offensive to clinch the deal when the opponent was on the ropes. Meanwhile, 'Uncle Henry' was re-assuring the increasingly nervous coterie of foreign policy geeks that the thoughtful Kushner was containing the impulsive president.

The Charm Offensive

Maybe Trump's intuition was working better than all the wonks in Washington. Kim Jong-un had proved his nuclear credentials and now he wanted to improve his relations with the outside world. He had stacked his bargaining chips and was ready to play the game of international poker. Kim had satisfied the military-first policy and his regime was relatively secure, and now he needed to bolster the economy and for that he had to work with other allies besides the Chinese. And he had to remove sanctions.

Behind the scenes, the North Koreans had been talking in depth to their southern compatriots. Seoul informed the White House that Kim Jong-un was 'eager' to meet Donald Trump. Moon Jae-in, the South Korean president, called this 'a miracle'. On 8 March 2018 the White House confirmed that the president would accept an invitation to meet the North Korean leader in the next few months. The White House also announced that 'in the meantime all sanctions and maximum pressure must remain'. The summit was scheduled for 12 June in Singapore. Then a joint military exercise between US forces and the South Koreans prompted the North Koreans to threaten to pull out from the Singapore meeting. Trump cancelled it anyway but reversed that decision a week later. Was all this shrewd brinkmanship or just chaotic indecision?

On 12 June 2018 Kim and Trump met in the five-star Capella Spa Hotel on Sentosa Island, Singapore. This was the first-ever meeting between leaders of the USA and North Korea. And the two alpha males seemed to get on. They both smiled and seemed relaxed with each other. The US president said that Kim was 'very smart' and 'a good negotiator'. Trump also said that he 'trusted' the North Korean dictator. This was Trump's classic mode of negotiation – he called it 'happy talk'.

They signed a joint statement, agreeing to security guarantees for North Korea, new peaceful relations, the de-nuclearization of the Korean peninsula, and follow-up negotiations between high-level officials. Both leaders also met separately with Lee Hsien Loong, the prime minister of Singapore. Kim even did a public walkabout to the delight of the media. The summit also included a vague agreement about North Korea returning the remains of about 7,000 PoW/MIA Americans. One month later North Korea sent fifty-five boxes to the US. They consisted of bone fragments but there was only one dog-tag ID, so it was almost impossible to identify any of the remains.

Immediately following the summit, President Trump announced that the American armed forces would discontinue 'provocative' joint military exercises with South Korea. The president also stated that he wished to bring America's soldiers back home from South Korea at some point but he emphasized that it was not part of the Singapore deal. When Trump announced – much to the surprise of his advisers – that the US would not engage in major annual exercises, this was a big concession. For what? Trump had given up a crucial component of southern deterrence. It was an invitation for Kim Jong-un – who had turned out to be a confident, able and even self-deprecating negotiator – to ask Washington to remove all its 30,000 troops as part of full normalization and a final peace deal. That might have been an impulsive Trump offer or a shrewd face-saving way of Kim giving up at least some of his nukes in exchange for a way out of sanctions.

In July 2018 the US secretary of state, Mike Pompeo, visited North Korea to a muted welcome. The local media complained about the 'gangster-like demands of de-nuclearization'. The UN's International Atomic Energy Authority stated that North Korea was continuing its nuclear programme and Trump said that Pompeo's next visit was cancelled. Nevertheless, Pompeo followed up with a second visit to Pyongyang and he seemed to establish a rapport with his North Korean counterpart, Ri Yong-ho. This time the regime's media went overboard about 'a new era of peace'. Even the ubiquitous anti-American posters in central Pyongyang disappeared.

North-Korean-US relations appeared to be as mercurial as their leaders.

In September President Trump commended Kim Jong-un at the UN General Assembly. The US president praised him for ceasing nuclear testing and for dismantling several military facilities as well as releasing some American hostages/prisoners in North Korea and also for returning the remains of American PoWs and Missing-in-Action soldiers. Trump re-iterated, however, that sanctions would remain in place until de-nuclearization actually happened.

A curious incident in Madrid

At around 16.00 on 22 February 2019 – right between the Singapore meeting and the subsequent Hanoi summit – a radical political group calling itself 'Free Joseon' broke into the two-storey North Korean embassy in Madrid. The masked and armed gang beat up the diplomats inside and took hard drives and documents with them. They numbered ten men who spoke Korean. The raiders spent about five hours in the embassy allowing for a detailed search; eventually the police arrived, alerted by a female member of the embassy staff who had hidden and then managed to escape. One of the attackers, sporting a traditional North Korean lapel badge showing the leaders, pretended to be a staff member and explained that there was no problem. The police could not enter an embassy and stood guard outside. The raiders had already managed to disable some of the security systems and then brazenly drove away in the CD-plated embassy cars from a rear garage. They switched cars and reached Portugal and, from there, flew to the USA, where they handed over to the FBI a treasure trove of data, especially about North Korean encryption software. Allegedly – because the FBI made no comment.

The Spanish police and intelligence services appeared embarrassed and reticent to talk. Eventually they said that the suspects, who had escaped, were from the US, Mexico and South Korea. Privately, the Spanish police briefed the media that they suspected – but could not prove – that it was a CIA operation. The CIA also privately responded, saying the high profile of the clumsy attack at such a sensitive diplomatic juncture could not have been ordered by Washington – despite the chaos in the White House. Later, intelligence briefings suggested that the US would not hit embassies; they had the largest number in the world and this could encourage copycat attacks. The attack on the US embassy in Tehran had left the most bitter of legacies. Also, it was said that the US would not want to upset a key NATO ally such as Spain.

Free Josean was founded in 2017 as Cheollima Civil Defense and was also called the Provisional Government of Free Korea. The word 'Cheollima' relates to a mythical winged horse commonly portrayed in Asian mythology, which has been featured in material by the North Korean government to promote economic development. 'Joseon' refers to the Korean dynasty that lasted for five centuries. The organization came to prominence in 2017 when it said they were protecting Kim Jong-un's nephew, Kim Han-sol, whose father Kim Jong-nam was assassinated with a nerve agent at Kuala Lumpur airport in Malaysia.

Renamed Free Joseon in March 2019, it claimed responsibility for the Madrid attack. As the Trump dialogue with Kim continued, Free Joseon issued a statement:

> Millions starved to death, hundreds of thousands of citizens in concentration camps, and hundreds of foreigners kidnapped and assassinated, will attest that, unfortunately, the regime in Pyongyang has never acted in good faith and only seeks to stall while it continues to proliferate weapons of mass destruction and commit mass atrocities. Regretfully, these empty gestures by the Kim regime serve only to deceive the world and empower an immoral criminal regime.

This statement, released on 30 June 2019, reads as though it could have been written in Washington. Perhaps it was. The Free Joseon movement, allegedly comprising some escapees from North Korea, was probably created by the CIA, although the National Intelligence Service of South Korea might have been equally involved. American money and a guiding hand can be seen in a number of similarly clandestine operations such as Free North Korean Radio, based in Seoul.

Kim Hyok-chol had been the ambassador in the North Korean embassy in Spain until he was asked to leave by Madrid. He had high-level connections with both intelligence and the nuclear programme – apparently he was tasked with supervising sanctions-busting in Europe. Intelligence sources indicated that the Madrid embassy contained a lot of important data, especially decryption protocols. The CIA, if they were the main drivers, may well have subcontracted the operation to their South Korean counterparts, perhaps with the connivance of Spanish security agencies. Watergate was a bungled raid at night; the embassy raid in broad daylight produced, apparently, a motherload of intelligence, and no one was badly hurt. Free Joseon did look suspiciously like a CIA front. The raid on the embassy appeared professional enough but free Korea was still a long way off.

The Hanoi summit et al

The two presidential chest-beating alphas met in Hanoi on 27/28 February 2019. The media and Kim Jong-un had expected a signing ceremony on 28 February. It was called off because neither could agree on a deal, even a cosmetic one. Kim returned and started to rebuild his long-range rockets at the Sohae Launch Facility. Trump's charm had failed. After the second meeting, the US president said that he had talked with Kim about the US hostage, Otto Warmbier, who was returned brain-dead to the US: 'He tells me he didn't know about it and I will take him at his word.' Trump took that on trust, but not the eternal promise of de-nuclearization. Neither the 'happy talk' nor the 'maximum pressure' had leveraged Kim from his mental bunker to the real negotiating table. The removal of sanctions was important but not as vital as Kim's military deterrence.

Kim was obviously miffed by the Hanoi failure. He was said to be angry because the US delegation confronted him with evidence of weapons facilities that his government had never acknowledged. According to South Korean media reports, Kim executed his envoy for US affairs and former unlucky ambassador in Madrid, Kim Hyok-chol, and four of his assistants were shot by firing squad for allegedly spying for the US. Other officials who had worked on the summit had been despatched to a prison camp.

But the game was not up. In April 2019 Trump tweeted that a third summit would be good (presumably for world peace and for his own re-election prospects). On 26 June it was announced that a third meeting would take place, after Trump said he had received a letter from Kim that he described as 'beautiful'. North Korea also issued a photo of Kim reading, it was said, a letter from Trump. Kim was quoted as saying that the letter was 'excellent' and he described Trump as 'the supreme leader of the United States'. The two leaders were publicly displaying their rapprochement but behind the scenes no tangible agreements had been hammered out. This was twitter and epistolary diplomacy without any real substance – this played to the egos of both showmen.

Then came a super-gimmick and spectacular photo op. On 30 June 2019, Trump met with Kim and the president of South Korea, Moon

Jae-in, at the DMZ and the US president briefly crossed the border line into the North Korean side. The Donald was the first sitting president to enter North Korea. Both Jimmy Carter and Bill Clinton had visited North Korea but they had already left office. Obama hadn't tried to personally engage Kim directly. When Trump walked into the north Kim said in English: 'It's good to see you again.' Both crossed into the north and then both returned over the demarcation line into the south. During their chat, Trump invited Kim to the White House although the Donald was realistic enough to say afterwards that it was not likely to happen in the near future.

Jared Kushner's secret diplomacy was also revealed. He had travelled to Pyongyang with his wife Ivanka to set up the continuing summitry. Footage of Ivanka's meeting with Kim was broadcast on North Korean TV. Clearly the daughter had inherited some of her father's showmanship. For Jared Kushner's emulation of 'Uncle Henry' if Pyongyang was 2019, then 2020 might herald, finally, an American diplomatic triumph in Jerusalem. Or was it be eternally delayed as in the Jewish prayer, 'Next Year in Jerusalem'?

Chapter 12

Renewed Friendship: Russia

N orth Korea was once firmly a part of the communist bloc before it went its own idiosyncratic way as a semi-Confucian rogue state run by a very un-communist hereditary 'monarchy'. Kim Il-sung had tried hard to play off both sides in the Sino-Soviet split that led eventually to a shooting war on their borders. Russia and North Korea also shared a border of just eleven miles that was formed in 1860 when Tsar Alexander II gained territory ceded from China in the Convention of Peking. After the Second World War, Moscow administered the north from 1945 to 1948. Soviet aid was then crucial during the Korean War, especially the provision of badly needed pilots. Kim Il-sung visited Moscow five times and had once been a major in the Red Army. Military and civilian nuclear assistance continued, as did food aid but, under the reformist leadership of Mikhail Gorbachev, Moscow began to favour South Korea's economic dynamism. The last delivery of MiG-29s to Pyongyang was made in 1989.

North Korea also benefited from extensive economic assistance from the USSR. The official figure was that the Soviet Union had helped build ninety-three factories and industrial plants in the north. Before the end of the Cold War about 60 per cent of North Korea's trade was with the USSR. Moscow provided petrol to North Korea at knock-down prices. And, even after the fall of the USSR, Moscow sent large amounts of humanitarian aid especially during the hungry years of the 1990s.

In the post-USSR period, during the Yeltsin reign, Moscow temporarily abandoned the North Korean begging bowls in favour of trade with South Korea. In 1996 Moscow-Pyongyang relations thawed a little, however. Nevertheless, the end of ideological ties and North Korea's inability to pay international market prices made the hermit state an unattractive option. But with the estrangement of Russia from the West relations picked up, not least on the old logic that my enemy's enemy is my friend. When Putin came to power three years later, Kim Jong-il made the Thatcherite assessment that now there was a Russian leader with whom he could do business. Vladimir Putin visited the North Korean capital in July 2000, the first Russian leader to do so, and they reached a new bilateral agreement, the first international document signed by Kim Jong-il as leader of the DPRK. In 2006, however, Russia supported the UN Security Council resolution condemning North Korea's missile tests. Relations soured almost completely in May 2009 after the first nuclear test. Russia genuinely feared an outbreak of nuclear war in the region, so Moscow imposed new sanctions, especially after Pyongyang threatened to attack South Korea. Russia joined in the US-led plan to check DPRK vessels that were possibly carrying WMD-related equipment. By June 2009 both Russia and China supported the extended UN sanctions but the two old allies of North Korea rejected any deployment of force to back sanctions. In March 2010 Russia clamped down on any financial and educational organizations that might have been facilitating the nuclear programme on Russian soil. Moscow also condemned North Korean attacks on South Korea, for example the artillery bombardment of Yeonpyeong island.

Kim Jong-il continued to court Putin, however. One positive outcome for the DPRK was the Russian decision to write off 90 per cent of North Korea's $11 billion debt to Moscow. The Russians knew that the debt would not be paid, but Moscow hoped that the write-off would grease the Russian request to build a trans-Korean railway and electricity and gas pipelines through the north to South Korea. In September 2013 Russia and North Korea completed a 54-kilometre rail link from Hasan in Russia to North Korea's Special Economic Zone in Rason. Given the state of tension on the peninsula the rail, oil and gas links remained, literally, a pipe dream. North Korea sent a delegation to the 2014 Winter Olympic Games in Sochi, although not a team of competitors.

In April 2019 Kim Jong-un journeyed in his armoured train to Vladivostok for his first-ever meeting with Putin. The train's arrival was greeted with a military orchestra. The trip, not coincidentally, was soon after the collapse of the second summit, in Hanoi, with Donald Trump. The key item on the agenda was obviously the nuclear stand-off. Unlike Washington, Moscow wanted to accept the status quo: de-nuclearization was seen as an unrealistic goal, so the Kremlin wanted to talk to Kim, not least to stabilize the dangerous situation.

But other issues were on the table as well. The meeting on the campus of Russia's Far Eastern University was intended to display the long friendship between the two nations. Champagne toasts and Russian folk dancing were intended to enhance the cordiality, especially after the failed summit with the Americans. The two leaders exchanged suitable action-man presents. Kim gave Putin a golden sword; Putin contributed a sabre (plus a tea service suitable for use on Kim's favourite armoured train).

Kim wanted some help with his sanctions-battered economy and Moscow intended to act as a counterweight to American influence. Putin did not want to be left out of the big game that had been previously dominated by the USA and China. Yet President Putin was careful not to step on the toes of either of the two superpowers. He emphasized his role as a possible facilitator with both. He would be discussing his talks with Kim during a forthcoming visit to Beijing for the Belt and Road Forum, he said. Putin would also chat to his friend in the White House. He said he would discuss the summit 'frankly and openly with the American leadership. Russia is always transparent, there are no conspiracies,' Putin said at his press conference in Vladivostok.

Other items on the agenda were the 10,000 North Korean labourers who were due to leave because of the UN sanctions. Labour abroad has always been a major source of hard currency for Pyongyang. Russian trade with North Korea was small, just $34 million in 2018, mostly because of sanctions. Russia wanted greater access to minerals, especially rare metals. Kim needed Russian investment to modernize the dilapidated Soviet-built plants, railways and other infrastructure.

Both leaders secured some photo-op kudos from the summit – both were seen as players on the international stage, especially important for the former pariah of Pyongyang. Beyond that, little was achieved. Kim wanted money in the form of aid. The overwhelming sense in Moscow was that North Korea had been an unreliable and unmanageable state, so it would not pour money in as it once did, for ideological, not commercial, reasons. Moscow would at best turn the occasional blind eye to minor sanctions busting. Putin's Russia was also a sanctions-battered state and could ill afford to donate charity to the endless pit of North

Korean economic mismanagement. Putin was more interested in holding his own with China and collecting brownie points with South Korea and, above all, Trump.

Trainspotting

Kim Jong-un's railway trip mirrored the one made by his father who met Putin in Vladivostok in 2002 and once completed a 12,000-mile round trip to Moscow on the same train. Kim Jong-il's fear of flying and paranoia about security made the big green bulletproof train a useful refuge. It was ironic that, in December 2011, Kim Jong-il died – presumably from natural causes – while on a domestic train trip.

Trains have often been favoured by royalty and global leaders, especially dictators, because of their speed, security and the convenience to accommodate extensive office facilities as well as personal luxuries within one highly mobile location. Kim Il-sung used a train as his headquarters during the Korean War. After the war he built numerous secure palaces, some underground, many of which were directly accessed by train or at least a nearby station – some of which could be reached only by private trains. The country has a special first-class system except that only three people – the Kims – have been labelled as first class. The DPRK boasts dozens of first-class stations reserved almost exclusively for the leader's use. The station roofs are camouflaged in green to make them more difficult to spot through satellite imagery. At ground level the buildings are unmarked but heavily armed guards patrol them and they are enclosed by high walls. Yongsun Station, on the northern outskirts of Pyongyang, has been a major first-class station used by the leader or sometimes to bring very elite members of the party to visit him at another station or palace. In the train hierarchy the royal Kim trains always come first. Then come goods trains. As in the UK, the passenger services always come last.

The leader's train is usually pulled by two engines. Green trains with a distinctive yellow line comprise a fleet of ninety special railway carriages that can be operated as six separate personal trains. Security was augmented after a 2004 explosion on the track in Ryongchon on the border with China. The explosion could have been an accident caused by a train loaded with oil and chemicals hitting power lines. It happened three hours after the leader's train passed through the area. Rumour mills went into overdrive about an assassination attempt, possibly masterminded by the diabolical CIA.

The possibility of an American-led decapitation attempt meant that trains switch routes and various false-flag leadership trains abound. CIA and South Korean tracking of the trains is therefore made more difficult. The trains tend to travel at under 40 mph (partly because of the weight of the armour) and work in fleets of three. The first train goes ahead to check the safety and integrity of the track. A little later – it varies from twenty minutes to an hour – the train carrying the leader follows the pathfinder. A third train carries additional security details and communications kit. Once the itinerary is confirmed the area is cleared twenty-four hours before the three trains set off.

The North Korean leaders have been fond of train-travelling extensively abroad as they could connect with China and Russia – while allowing for a gauge change. A second train would have to carry wheels and axles of other gauges. This was how, in 1974, Kim Il-sung visited nearly every socialist country in Eastern Europe via China and Russia. Kim Jong-il's train had approximately twenty-two carriages, not least with room for kitchens for his epicurean tastes – the best French wines, and regular stops to collect live lobsters. The kitchens were capable of serving Russian, Chinese, Korean, Japanese and French cuisines.

In 2011 Kim Jong-il travelled nearly 3,000 miles to Russia to meet President Dmitry Medvedev – when he and his boss, Putin, 'castled' (to translate the Russian expression, *rokirovka*, for the chess move). They swapped jobs to allow Putin to come back later as president so as to get around the term limitations.

Kim Jong-un and his wife trained to China to meet President Xi Jinping. This was the first time the Great Successor had left the country after taking power in 2011. Kim had renovated the trains since his father's day. He is an Apple addict and so the communications were Americanized. The leather armchairs were re-upholstered in pink. Most flamboyantly, a red-carpeted ramp was erected inside one carriage in case an appropriate reception committee was lacking. During the last few long train journeys Kim Jong-un would smoke heavily although his ever-present sister-PA would run around after him and would loyally hold out a crystal ash-tray.

This was such a long way from the original austere socialist lifestyle preached by the Korean Workers' Party that his grandfather had formed.

Putin and Trump

If China was reluctant to bring the DPRK properly to heel, then Putin could – perhaps. Moscow had less leverage but Putin may have had the right angles as well as the strategic impulse. Russia had been invaded numerous times from the West, with the Germans doing it twice in a generation. The Far East, Siberia et al, was underpopulated, not least compared with the teeming Chinese population next door. The Soviets had fought the People's Liberation Army along the frozen Ussuri river where Chinese Manchuria meets the Russian Far East. The conflict went on for seven months in 1969 and Moscow war-gamed to take out the embryonic Chinese nuclear programmes if the fighting had escalated.

Putin had marked out the Far East for major development, not least of mineral resources. So the threat of regional nuclear war with North Korea seriously concerned the Russian leadership. Putin had played a weak hand very well – Russia was a pocket superpower compared with the Chinese or Americans. NATO, for example, spent ten times more on the military than even Putin's expanded defence programme. In short, Putin had a lot of incentives to work with the Americans to try to contain Pyongyang.

During his presidential campaign, Trump bigged up the Russian president. It was the talk of Washington that Putin had something on Trump, making him servile; a sort of latter-day *Manchurian Candidate*. Some blamed the 'pee-tapes' when Russian intelligence had allegedly filmed Trump indulging in unusual sex acts in a Moscow hotel during a beauty pageant the American businessman was involved with. The biggest question was whether Russia had been involved in electronic dirty tricks favouring Trump during his electoral battle with Hillary Clinton. This led to what Trump dubbed a witch-hunt by the FBI that threatened to end in impeachment proceedings. The Donald constantly denied any Russian collusion and yet when Trump met Putin in Helsinki in July 2018 he behaved like 'a beaten dog', to use Steve Bannon's telling phrase. It was a disaster similar to Jack Kennedy's first meeting with Nikita Khrushchev.

Here were two narcissistic cult-leader-type presidents who had real populist talents but Putin was far, far cleverer. In a desperate press conference where Trump seemed utterly humbled after a long one-on-one meeting – with no officials present, only interpreters – Trump dug himself deeper and deeper into a pit of humiliation while Putin stood next to him, just watching – 'the coolest cat who ever swallowed a canary' in author Michael Wolff's phrase. Steve Bannon also realized clearly that it was as terrible as Custer's defeat at the Little Big Horn. Recognizing Putin's mastery, Bannon said: 'God, Putin is a *badass.*'

Trump seemed unaware of his massive cock-up; it led to the most severe questioning of his mental capacity by friends and enemies alike. And yet if Putin could help Trump reach a good deal with the Little Rocket Man then all three could come out of the Korean imbroglio smelling of roses. And some sort of peace might ensue.

The Future of Suspicious Minds

The symbols of the North Korean regime are the conventional communist ones of hammer and sickle but a calligraphy brush was also added. They represent industry, farming and culture. The original socialist ideals have not been achieved, however. While the country is not a completely failed state, the Kims definitely have presided over a failed revolution. By a mix of a little pragmatism and a lot of oppression as well as relentless indoctrination of the general population, the state's elite families maintain their almost feudal grip on power. Nearly everyone expected the DPRK to collapse under the weight of its own stubborn, corrupt and egregiously incompetent system. And many outsiders expected this to happen when Kim Jong-un succeeded his father in 2011. Instead, the regime has not only survived but, by its lights, has begun to prosper. The young leader has pulled off a remarkable transformation. From being a joke, a pariah and a monster, he has somehow managed to persuade some of the most powerful people in the world to treat him as a normal head of a legitimate state. In no small measure the wackiness of the American president has helped Kim Jong-un look affable, rational and sensible, not least by comparison.

Vladimir Putin always understood that the DPRK could not give up its nukes and survive. Saddam and Gaddafi were too recent and too gory examples of what happens if dictators end up nuclear-naked. Washington has always wanted North Korea to get rid of its nukes in exchange for economic goodies and some security assurances. In the North Korean perspective this is almost impossible by definition. Only the nukes could be the ultimate guarantor as the UK, France and Israel, great allies of Washington, demonstrated by their own expensive nuclear deterrents. The USA also turned something of a blind eye to Pakistan's and India's nuclear proliferation. The one exception was South Africa, a very special case – and the US and UK intelligence agencies made sure that all the apartheid weapons, materials and secrets were removed before the black nationalists, old friends of Moscow, took command.

Pyongyang's road to international acceptance has been long and winding. Kim Il-sung manipulated Russia and China, almost like an emperor demanding tribute. Stalin personally sent an armoured limousine while Mao sent a train and carriages. The DPRK slowly developed international relations with non-communist countries in the 1980s and forged new ties with socialist governments, in Vietnam, for example, after the collapse of the USSR. By the time of the Obama administration, the hermit kingdom was certainly less of a pariah state. The USA has not recognized the regime. Nevertheless, North Korea eventually established diplomatic relations with 166 countries and maintained embassies in forty-seven states. The most symbolic relationship has been with South Korea; in September 2018 at a joint media conference in Pyongyang, the President of South Korea, Moon Jae-in, and the northern supremo, Kim Jong-un, agreed to turn the peninsula into 'a land of peace without nuclear weapons and nuclear threats'. Kim Jong-un was starting to act as though he was chasing a Nobel Peace Prize while keeping maybe 200,000 people in Nazi-style concentration camps.

One of the most important aspects of understanding the DPRK's survival is also to appreciate fully the difference between perspectives in Washington and Seoul. North Korea's highly provocative nuclear diplomacy and missile testing sometimes make senior Chinese leaders apoplectic, so it is no wonder that a series of American presidents also grew increasingly wary of Pyongyang's dangerous and repressive regime. South Koreans, however, take an Asian, Confucian and kith-and-kin view. South Koreans see a pitiable renegade brother, estranged by an accident of history in which the USA was partly culpable. South Koreans in general do not believe that the northerners would use their nuclear weapons unless they are backed into a corner and forced to do so for regime survival. South Koreans are often more afraid of the American policy of regime change that could provoke Pyongyang into an Armageddon spasm.

And yet the DPRK remains a potent risk for South Korea and Japan as well as the wider region, let alone the continental USA, if the great dictator actually lets rip with his ICBMs. The DPRK's habit of taking risks, the additional emphasis on non-nuclear conventional and asymmetric warfare, especially its advanced cyber capabilities, plus its numerous SF forces and chemical weapons, must never be underestimated. It is also a super-mafia state with massive international syndicates operating people-trafficking and drug-smuggling, money laundering (often of fake US dollars) and illegal arms dealing in both nuclear and conventional weapons.

Kim Jong-un might make some obvious cosmetic concessions by blowing up a defunct nuclear plant or two but his real power may be in cyberspace. The armed forces run an elite unit called Bureau 121. Clever youngsters are recruited to fight in the new secret war. They can do anything from malware to ransomware and penetrating gambling sites, for example, so long as they meet their targets. Many base themselves in Russia, China and Malaysia where the internet connections are far better. They make big salaries while keeping some for themselves and remitting the rest to Pyongyang, sometimes directly to the leader's private accounts. The Bureau in 2016 stole $8 million from Bangladesh's central bank and the FBI called it 'the largest cyber-heist in history'. It was also blamed for the 2017 WannaCry virus in 150 countries; the British NHS suffered badly from this attack, for example. South Korea in 2019 was hit by 1.5 million cyber-attacks per day; Pyongyang has also hit numerous Japanese companies. The NATO treaty obligations require a response if a fellow member is attacked. That is how Russia is deterred, in theory. But what constitutes an attack when a cyber strike is invisible and totally deniable? If this is 'war', can we ever have peace again?

In trying to get the North Koreans to curb their criminal diplomacy and above all to give up their cherished sword, their nuclear weapons, it is ironic that the most unconventional of all American leaders, in dealing with the most unconventional of Asian leaders, fell victim to utterly conventional thinking. For example, that nukes could be bought with deals. Trump has made many mistakes regarding North Korea. One of the most famous was promising to stop the annual US–South Korean exercises because they were 'provocative'. John Bolton, when he became National Security Adviser, tried to rein in his president. The much-vaunted attempt to bribe Kim Jong-un to give up his nuclear weapons by lifting sanctions was never going to succeed but Trump ignored Bolton's advice by meeting the dictator in the DMZ. This was a huge boost for Kim's prestige. Then he demonstrated his gratitude by defiantly continuing to test his missiles. Bolton was sacked in the high summer of 2019, however. Besides the inevitable failure to secure the grand deal with Pyongyang, the Venezuelan government did not bend the knee to Yankee threats either. American troops remain in Afghanistan in 2019; a possible deal with the Taliban was the catalyst if not the cause of the final rift between Bolton and Trump. No arms control treaty with Moscow has emerged. Above all, in late 2019 the long-impending war between the USA and its allies against Iran looks far closer than ever. Trump's deal-making looked rather threadbare.

And the most crucial failure was Trump's dealings with Iran. President Obama had helped to secure a six-nation deal to curb the progress of Iran's nuclear weapons programme. It was flawed in many ways, not least the failure to curb Tehran's many destabilizing military actions in Iraq, Syria and Lebanon. Its missile programme was untouched as well. And yet the deal did seem to stop or at least slow down Iran's rapid march to nuclear-weapon status which in turn would have set off an arms race in the region, starting with its arch enemy Saudi Arabia going nuclear as well. Trump ripped up the deal without an apparent fall-back strategy. Besides angering Tehran, Trump's unilateralism alienated the other members of the deal, especially France and the UK. The impact on Pyongyang is shatteringly obvious. Why should Kim Jong-un make any sort of deal with President Trump – a deal that could be shredded just like the Iranian de-nuclearization agreement?

Why no collapse?

How on earth did the North Korean regime survive despite the loss of allies and mass starvation? Why didn't it collapse like the USSR or modernize like China? It was conventional wisdom that the country would inevitably give in, not least to sanctions – which was part again of Trump's conventional thinking. The Spartan nationalism of the DPRK, however, was more likely to be entrenched, not undermined, by foreign economic pressures and military threats.

When the 'troubles' – the demands for democracy – started in the Soviet bloc, the DPRK press always liked to stress the genetic superiority of the Koreans, especially the northerners who had not been mollycoddled by capitalism as in the south. The Eastern Europeans and the Chinese weren't as strong by nature or as disciplined. They had deviated from the true path of socialism. Nor did they have genius leadership like the Kims. Now if you believe the great leaders do not defecate or urinate like ordinary mortals then you would believe anything. And many in the DPRK – after endless brainwashing in school, the armed forces and in the dogmatic media – were true believers.

In 2018 the Monty Python star, Sir Michael Palin, made a TV film in North Korea. He was talking to one of his female minders about the differences between their two countries.

'Our way of life is based on freedom of speech,' Palin said. 'People can be as rude as they like about their leaders. In my country we are able to criticize our leaders if they do something wrong and, like any human beings, they frequently do make mistakes.'

The state guide immediately came back: 'That's what makes us so different. Our leaders are very great. They are not individuals. They represent the masses, so we cannot criticize ourselves, can we?'[1]

The North Koreans had no choice but to accept official explanations for obvious catastrophes, most notably the lack of food in a socialist paradise. US sanctions had some credibility as an excuse (though of course America also provided a great deal of humanitarian aid). Then the DPRK citizens were told that the government was stockpiling food to feed the starving South Koreans masses on the blessed day of re-unification. Far less plausible, but even the most sceptical of North Koreans had to keep schtum, even within the family. After the mass famine of the 1990s, the claims of socialist plenty became even more preposterous.

> The farmers ... neglected the collective fields for their private 'kitchen gardens' next to their houses or small steep plots carved out of the side of uncultivated mountain slopes. Driving through the North Korean countryside you could see clearly the contrast between the private gardens bursting with vegetables, bean poles soaring skyward, vines drooping with pumpkins, next to the collective fields with their stunted, haphazard rows of corn that had been planted by so-called volunteers doing their patriotic duty. The

people who stood the most to lose were the city folk who had no land on which to grow their own food.[2]

So why didn't the masses revolt? Nobody could bring change or fight from within; not while the military and Pyongyang elite were fed and as long as the Kim family members held their nerve. Many North Koreans escaped when they could, despite the savage retribution inflicted on their remaining families – possibly for ever. Others were whipped into line by the ubiquitous social controls and security police. The Kims killed all those who wanted reform. Most famously Kim Jong-un executed his own uncle because he was seen to favour some reforms on the Chinese model. Yet oppression, propaganda and brainwashing can never provide the entire answer. The survival of the regime has been based on a number of more subtle factors. Many did suffer but a small elite did well – they were very generously rewarded for their loyalty. Crucially, there has been some improvement and the improvement can be seen by the general population – the markets, for example, are everywhere. People have more goods and more and better food. A farmer who maybe ate meat twice a year might now eat it once or twice a month. That is why if you meet any North Koreans outside the country, they will always opt for the best steak, if you offer them a meal. So, small improvements, and a little less oppression perhaps, plus the southern sunshine policies and joint enterprise zones and unified sports teams, allow people to look forwards, to hope and believe in a better future. People will usually believe what they want to believe; that is a basic premise of all propaganda. Above all, in the north – as in the south – a strong sense of national pride has emerged. It is genuine in both countries.

An example of hope can be found in Wonsan. In June 2019 the DPRK allowed a small group of journalists to visit the resort complex there. It has hotels, funfairs, boardwalks and water parks designed to bring in about one million tourists a year. A *Sunday Times* journalist, Philip Sherwell, wrote this:

Wonsan is where Kim's dual priorities for regime survival – economic development and national defence – come together. He has a fun-and-guns-in-the-sun strategy that is pivotal to both his pride and his purse strings.[3]

What happens next?

Predicting what the Kim dictatorship will do next is a risky game. Both the current DPRK and US leaders are in an unpredictable category all of their own. Anything's possible, even a proper peace deal. Unlikely, but possible.

Despite the relative failure of the Trump-Kim dialogues so far, the peninsula in 2019 is far less dangerous; there is far less chance of war by design or accident. The realities have changed little but the mood music has become more mellow. The future will be dictated by realpolitik not ethics, however. The UN special commission into North Korea's human rights abuses found that these violations were not 'mere excesses of the state' but 'essential components' of its totalitarian system. 'The gravity, scale and nature of these violations reveal a state that does not have any parallel in the contemporary world', the commission concluded in a landmark 2014 report. It recommended that Kim Jong-un be referred to the International Criminal Court to face charges against humanity. The last time this was recommended in the case of a sitting head of state, Omar al-Bashir of Sudan, it was largely ignored.[4] Kim Jong-un is unlikely to face his day in court – even if the regime collapses. Nuremberg trials won't happen for the ruling dynasty. Kim will jump on his green train and escape to China or Russia.

The north is not likely to repeat an invasion of the south. China would not let that happen. Beijing would probably like a change in leadership to someone who is not related to the three Kims. It has been suggested in the worst days of anti-Kim coldness that Kim Jong-un could be politely asked to stay on in Beijing after his medical treatment but for a very long time. That is very unlikely.

Unification?

The drive for re-unification has been a key component of the DPRK's propaganda and policy. In the south, support for re-unification, especially among the young, has waned. According to a 2017 poll published by the Korea Institute for National Unification, just over 72 per cent of South Koreans in their 20s believed that uniting north and south was unnecessary. Other polling of older South Koreans make it plain that the vast majority do not want their lifestyles to suffer just to accommodate the bankrupt north. In 2017 some 30,000 North Korean refugees were living in South Korea. They were generally smaller in stature, less healthy, less well-educated and suffered from discrimination. South Koreans tended to associate them with laziness, drunkenness and being too reliant on state handouts. Generally, at best, they were regarded like the Irish in England in the 1950s, as boozy, workshy and feckless. This type of prejudice often makes younger South Koreans wonder if unification is possible or even desirable. As older South Koreans die out and their relations in the north do too, and with them memories of the pre-Korean War peninsula, re-unification has become a slightly romantic aspiration and not any kind of possible political reality in the near future.

The sunshine policy was predicated on creating conditions for eventual re-unification. And yet many more conservative South Koreans saw the policy – and especially sending so much aid – as nothing more than appeasement that allowed the regime more time to continue to persecute its own citizens. Isolation would lead to eventual collapse and finally absorption by the south, some argued. And yet practical proposals for possible re-unification continued to be part of the political debate in the south, epitomized by the long debate about a specific 'unification tax' paid by individuals and businesses. In addition, there have been numerous plans for a political confederation, preceded by a Korean Economic Community modelled on the European Union (though a rapid Pyongyang 'Brexit' could easily be imagined). The DPRK has considered similar solutions. As far back as 1973 it touted the idea of a 'Federal Republic of Koryo'. The name comes from a kingdom that helped to unite and rule the peninsula from 918 to 1392. This revived traditional structure would represent all the Korean people at the UN, for example.

The obvious comparisons, Germany and Vietnam, have featured in numerous research proposals for unification. Both examples involved the amalgamation of communist states with capitalist entities. An obvious difference is, of course, the long conflict between the two Koreas. Germany did not lose millions of lives in a *civil* war. Also, the East Germans could see that the West Germans had a much better lifestyle, not least good retirement, social and health benefits as well as a strong civil society and democratic freedoms. It is unclear whether many North

Koreans are aware of any immediate benefits of re-unification. Even if they did have any views they would not be able to express them.

Koreans have always been an unusually homogenous people. In Germany the psychological division has been called the *die Mauer im Kopf* (the wall in the head) and it has caused many social and political problems. Germany was divided for forty years and there were some contacts, whereas Korea has been bisected for over seventy-two years and the north has been almost entirely quarantined from the south. At re-unification the East German population was about a third of the West German (around 60 million); the North Korean population is currently about half of South Korea's (51 million).

The costs of re-unification would be enormous – estimated at around $1 trillion US dollars under the best of circumstances over several decades. Higher estimates of $3 trillion have been suggested if the unification were to be chaotic and sudden. South Korea's annual GDP is around $2 trillion so the concern of many young South Koreans about the possible costs in lower living standards is understandable. The income per capita ratio was about 3:1 between the two Germanys; in Korea the disparity is about 22:1.

And yet provided the re-unity was relatively peaceful, a unified Korea could surpass all the current G7 countries, except the USA, within a few decades, according to a Goldman Sachs report. The young semi-skilled labour force and large amounts of natural resources from the north allied with the south's high tech, infrastructure and capital could create an amazing synthesis. Chinese entrepreneurs, never slow off the mark, have started buying up land and properties on their side of the North Korean border. A unified Korean state with a population of over 80 million could conjure up an economic miracle in a few decades. The unification of north and south Vietnam is more analogous and that war-ravaged country has developed considerably, not least by emulating much of the capitalism of its old enemy, the USA. In the longer term the greenback has triumphed where the B-52s failed conspicuously.

Rebuilding the north could cost a fortune, far more than the current status quo costs of regular aid and security measures. Unification could lead to millions of North Koreans moving south and causing the economy to stagnate or collapse. As in nearly all such matters, re-unification's success depends on how it is done.

It also depends on how the big neighbour reacts. Beijing has frequently been exasperated by the DPRK's bellicosity as well as the amount of aid it has sucked from its neighbour. Provided a unified Korea was not hostile to China, it could help boost regional prosperity. China could help ensure de-nuclearization on the South African model in exchange for the removal of US forces. A strong Korea, however, could inflame nationalism among the many Koreans in China as well as stoke up the various territorial disputes between Beijing and the Koreas. It has even been suggested that China could annex northern Korea to avoid extended instability. That would be unlikely except in very grave circumstances.

Peaceful unification under a democratic government has long been official US policy. The DPRK has very privately conceded that it has tolerated the US military presence and the DMZ, as it has helped to prevent another outbreak of war. It was not just the DPRK who wanted to go south; a go-north military faction has been influential at times in Seoul.

A unified Korea would have the largest number of trained military reservists in the world as well as the largest number of talented cyber warriors. Its combined military and economic strengths could become a Frankenstein's monster and dramatically shake up the balance of power in the region.

The Chinese conundrum

Most thinking about the future of the two Koreas is premised on the stability of the Big Brother next door: China. It used to be said that the USA was the arsenal of democracy; the big military parade in Beijing to celebrate, in September 2019, the 70th anniversary of the People's Republic of China suggested that China has become the arsenal of tyranny. China has moved almost seamlessly from Cultural Revolution to cultural amnesia. Power alone, not any ideology, seems revered in China, in a national denial of the crimes of its patriarch. It has been assumed that China will be the totalitarian top-dog superpower of the future. Russia is a parallel, if smaller, version. And yet China did not go through a period of political liberalization as happened after the fall of the USSR. Dramatic economic expansion in China has not brought dramatic political changes. The opposite has happened: the Chinese leader has become president for life and party cohesion and discipline have been tightened up. Persecution of religious minorities in China is widespread and the penal system is draconian. Despite the cultural genocide of the Uighurs in Xinjiang, China *has* changed, however. Thirty years before the 70th anniversary victory parade, pro-democracy protests in Tiananmen Square were met by tanks and machine-gun fire. Earlier, in Mao's time, the Great Leap Forward caused perhaps as many as 30 million peasants to starve to death. Today China is more like where South Korea stood in its US-backed authoritarian stage – it's not like the tough North Korean authoritarian rule of 2019.

China is an on-off partner with Washington in providing some curbs on the DPRK's nuclear adventurism. And yet Beijing's own military adventurism in the South China Sea, for example, could lead to a major conflict with America or its allies in the region. The key muscle-flexing of China is economic, however. Beijing, a member of the World Trade Organization for nearly two decades, has driven at breakneck speed its industrialization and economic growth, as well as creating a big hoard of US dollars. Trump has blamed this trade imbalance on 'unfair' Chinese practices and hence the 2019 US trade war. Chinese trade practices do have many faults, not least the notorious cases of industrial espionage regarding intellectual property rights as well as aggressive protectionism of its own domestic businesses. Nevertheless, Chinese integration into the world economy has been a big plus. In essence, Chinese savings allow American consumers to enjoy an artificially high standard of living.

Western states may be wary of Chinese economic and military prowess and its glaring disregard for human rights but it could be far worse if China collapses, and not just because of the possible impact of the removal of restraints on North Korea. At the same time as the victory parade in Beijing to celebrate the 70th anniversary of the Chinese Republic, Hong Kong was entering its seventeenth week of violent pro-democracy protests against the gradual erosion of the promise of 'one country, two systems' under which the territory was handed back by the UK in 1997. Then Hong Kong was a pocket economic superpower in its own right –

it comprised about one-fifth of the Chinese economy; now the ratio is 1: 32. Beijing is extremely reluctant – at the time of writing – to send in the People's Liberation Army to gain control of the streets in Hong Kong. That kind of iron fisted action would crash China's prestige, especially around the time of such a major anniversary.

The continuous and increasingly violent actions by police and protestors in Hong Kong are bound eventually to infect the republic as a whole. The assumption of permanent Chinese stability and the rise to the Number One position in the world may be questioned. (The Mandarin slang for the Chinese bid to 'to catch up and surpass' America is abbreviated to *ganchao.*) Many other factors, besides Hong Kong and the trade war with the USA, should be considered. The one-child policy, despite its recent relaxation, has meant that the workforce is shrinking and ageing. Also, the Chinese government has built up a massive domestic level of debt, despite its dollar reserves; the massive environmental damage due to its rapid industrialization will cost trillions to fix. (If there is *time* to fix it, the environmental lobby would say.) And, in the end, will the largest bourgeoisie in history, especially one which is so media savvy, endlessly tolerate one-party rule? Students of China's long and impressive saga will note the millennia of alternating periods of stability and chaos. Hong Kong's turmoil may indicate that the recent two or three decades of Chinese stability may be over.

*   *   *

Putting Chinese collapse aside, for the sake of analysis of North Korea's future let's assume *ceteris paribus.* So the likely conclusion – unless a major single incident occurs, a Chernobyl in North Korea, for example – is that north-south relations will gradually improve as trade increases with each other and with China and Japan. Sanctions will probably dwindle away – perhaps the regime makes some cosmetic changes – maybe blowing up some of the missiles, stopping any firings and nuclear tests and just keep the bombs 'in the basement'. The north cannot change unless there is regime change, but that probably can't come from the outside or the inside, for now. Maybe in a decade or two the Korean Workers' Party will finally decide that three great leaders from the same family are more than enough. More likely is a military coup with some generalissimo who could be strong enough to risk a 'grand bargain' with Seoul. An Asian Charles de Gaulle could give up the North Korean equivalent of Algeria. A reformed DPRK, united with the South, could be the powerhouse of Asia. There is some hope for the peninsula: after endless occupation, war and threats of war, the proud Korean people certainly *deserve* a better future.

The end of the DPRK?

Despite being a living political fossil that operates a zombie economy, the dynasty has somehow survived. That has been the theme of this book: far from being lunatics, the DPRK's coldblooded rulers have generally displayed very sane and determined survival strategies. As Andrei Lankov, the Russian expert on the regime, put it, they are 'perhaps the most ruthless and Machiavellian leaders in the world today'.[5]

They have played very trick in the book to effectively demand ransoms by nuclear blackmail and usually getting the money without ever doing anything so vulgar as paying their bills. They have been 'cheating and retreating' for decades and constantly 'selling the same horse twice', in hard-line American parlance. And yet all things must eventually end. Some sort of collapse, violently sudden or more peacefully gradual, must happen. We all know that foreign experts have been predicting the collapse of the regime since its inception. They have been wrong so far; but they will be right eventually.

South Korea does not want to pick up the entire trillion-dollar bill for rebuilding the dinosaur that is the northern economy. China will probably help, as will Japan and the USA and maybe even penurious Russia. Although German and Vietnamese re-unification has been studied extensively there has been insufficient practical preparation for what happens if Kim Jong-un dies tomorrow, perhaps by accidently falling under his train or by an assassin's bullet.

In the transformation in Eastern Europe and Russia a 'second society' took over. These were professional classes who tried to treat the communist regimes just like weather conditions. Unavoidable, but life went on despite them. These opponents had as little as they could to do with the communist oligarchy. That is not the same in North Korea. Numerous soft policies have been suggested. One well-trodden route is for foreign exchange students. In the 1960s some top Soviets studied in the USA and became senior, albeit quiet, reformers – even in the KGB. In the UK the London School of Economics as well as the Royal Military Academy Sandhurst have helped train generations of transitional leaders. The South Koreans have hoped that the tens of thousands of northerners who have worked in the now closed Kaesong SEZ will have tasted some fruits of capitalist prosperity. Balloons carrying leaflets may be a bit passé but radio broadcasts, DVDs and USB sticks as well as Chinese phones and computers have enabled many northerners to see what alternatives are on offer. Some NGOs believe that the 30,000 northerners living in South Korea should be put on more educational programmes. They are not true 'defectors' in that they mostly escaped starvation or prison, not changed sides for ideological reasons. They have mostly been ill-educated peasants, not rocket scientists. This is perhaps the worst legacy of the Kim dictatorship: generations of North Koreans have no proper understanding of what is happening in the outside world. When their time comes to take part in helping to run a liberalized North Korea or a unified peninsula, they will be strikingly unready for the future culture shock.

Putting Humpty Dumpty back together again will be very hard. Even if the fall of the Kim empire is relatively peaceful, what comes after could be worse for a long while. Millions of North Koreans with primitive skills can walk south in a day or two. But South Korea does not need much unskilled labour. The northerners will be exploited in the new capitalist market while, in the north, numerous con-artists and carpetbaggers from the south could take advantage of northern naivety by setting up, for example, numerous Ponzi schemes as proliferated in Eastern Europe. Land title deeds have been handed down for three generations among former refugee families in the south. Many are now successful and can afford smart lawyers to chase ownership of their seized northern lands. What will happen to the three to four hundred thousand core professional warriors, the special forces, in the northern army? Will they be disbanded as they were disastrously in Iraq after the American occupation? Will they become security guards or professional criminals if even the elite SF types don't make it into the new but inevitably smaller joint professional army?

To avoid the chaos as happened in the south after the American Civil War, or – in a rarely quoted example of re-unification – the killing fields and economic desert that is today's Yemen, perhaps a temporary confederation could emerge? Borders could be maintained not by machine guns as at present, but by visas and guards who say 'please'. De-Kimification could allow for a Truth and Reconciliation Commission on the South African model. To avoid hanging people upside down from lampposts, Kim and his immediate family could decamp to Macau under Chinese protection. The menfolk could indulge their favourite pastimes of chasing pretty young women and guzzling top-notch brandy along with fresh lobsters. Their millions stashed away in Macau and Switzerland could be returned to the treasury in Pyongyang.

North Korea has lasted over seventy-two years and is not likely to repeat that lengthy experience. But the Kim dynasty could survive a decade or more. So far, threats and bribes have not changed the regime much, nor can they be strong-armed into reform, so interim deals have to be done. In exchange for a lot of money, Kim Jong-un could go for a version of the so-called 'three noes': no more nukes, no better nukes and no proliferation. In effect this is what Kim Jong-un has announced during his talks with Donald Trump. The great dictator claims he has finished his nuclear deterrent programme, so he could stop and even get rid of a few nukes and missiles. He will never give them all up but a minimum deterrent would still work.

In the longer term the regime is not only damned, it is also doomed. Its intrinsically incurable and utterly failed socialist model has meant that the DPRK has completely lost not only the battle with South Korea but also with the modern world. Unless it somehow reforms itself, under a leader who is not part of the Kim dynasty, then the system must inevitably collapse – in days, weeks, months or years. Nobody knows. No matter how peaceful the reunification, it will still be messy, whether co-ordinated by the United Nations or administered by South Koreans with China and America holding their hands. And it will take many years to clear up the mess left by the Kims' misrule. The biggest victims of the failed revolutionaries in Pyongyang have been the North Korean people. The regime killed maybe three million of its own citizens because it started the 1950 war; it perhaps starved up to three million and possibly one million died in the gulags. Seven million killed directly and probably many more indirectly. The number killed is bigger than the Nazi Holocaust. And generations of North Korean survivors have had their lives blighted by the Kim dynasty. As they stand in the ruins of the People's Democratic Republic of Korea its citizens may, at last, have a chance to take a deep breath of freedom. That will be just the start of decades of recovery on the naturally beautiful but politically tragic peninsula.

Appendix

The North Korean Security Forces

The Korean People's Army

The army developed from guerrilla forces formed in the 1930s. During the Second World War the Korean Volunteer Army fought side by side with the Chinese communists who helped arm and train them. Kim Il-sung and some of his officers were trained in the USSR and fought alongside the Red Army. After the Soviet occupation in 1945 around 2,000 Koreans with military experience with Soviet forces were formed into a militia, initially to protect railways, but they evolved into a national army in August 1946, though the Korean People's Army was not formally activated until February 1948. The reversals of the Korean War led to China taking over command of the KPA. The attrition rate was heavy: the KPA suffered 290,000 casualties and 90,000 were taken prisoner.

Under the *Songun* policy, the armed forces are the central institution of the DPRK. The boss of the Korean Workers' Party, in 2019 Kim Jong-un, was given the rank of Supreme Commander and Chairman of the Central Military Commission. The Korean People's Army (KPA) consists of five branches:

- Ground Force
- Navy
- Air Force
- Strategic Rocket Force
- Special Operation Force

The KPA Ground Force is the de facto army. The People's Navy is organized into two fleets: one in the east is based at Toejo-dong and the fleet in the west is headquartered at Nampo. The overall HQ has always been in the capital. The navy also operates a weak air wing. The small, short-range vessels have not conducted joint operations, because they would have had to sail around the south of the peninsula and thus face the US-South Korean naval superiority in the region. The air force and air defence forces operate older equipment but the numerous types of artillery and surface-to-air missiles ensure a multi-layered air defence. The Strategic Rocket Force deploys the strategic missiles systems and the nuclear deterrent. The missiles are based on Soviet and Chinese models with some local adaptation. Special Forces number up to 200,000. By comparison, the British SAS might be able to field 400 men at short notice. The North Korean SF are well-trained, not least in infiltration into the south. In the 1960s, when large numbers of DPRK special forces were pushed across the DMZ, the Americans considered them the toughest opponents they had ever encountered.

The KPA is supported by around 190,000 paramilitary security troops, including police and border guards. The Worker and Peasant Red Guard, some well-armed, comprise around 5,700,000 personnel in cities and rural areas.

Doctrine

The original Soviet tradition of large-scale mechanized conventional warfare was modified by the Maoist concept of people's war. Some infantry units are mechanized but most are armed with lighter weapons and the emphasis is on night fighting in smaller groups. In the mid-1960s some of the forces were structured for insurgency roles after infiltration into the south. The forces were re-organized after the failure of the so-called Second Korean war (1966–69). The KPA maintains a forward threat of possible invasion of the south as well as defence in depth. Around 70 per cent of the ground forces and perhaps 50 per cent of the navy and air force are deployed within 100 kilometres of the DMZ. These forward forces work in a network that has more than 4,000 underground facilities and hardened artillery sites. Probably the rest of the country has another 11,000 underground facilities. Despite the nuclear deterrent, and the manpower size, it could be argued that economic disasters have undermined morale as well as the standard of training and equipment. Conscript troops on guard duties in urban areas often appear to be wearing uniforms of the wrong size and many don't even have socks. Often the lack of fuel has slashed training schedules. But the DPRK remains a potent threat for South Korea and Japan, based on its habit of taking risks, the emphasis on conventional and asymmetric warfare, especially its advanced cyber capabilities, plus its numerous SF forces, nukes and chemical weapons. The DPRK forged a new doctrinal emphasis and structures to create smaller, more mobile ground forces, long-range artillery and use of conventional missiles, 'electronic intelligence warfare' and the beefing up of the SF.

The KPA has sometimes showed flexibility, despite the dead hands of the politicians at the top and commissars in the ranks. The military planners examined in depth US operations in the Gulf Wars and Kosovo and began a series of reviews that stressed asymmetric warfare as a way of countering any major engagement with US and South Korean forces. New tanks were introduced, notably the *Chonma-ho* (a T-62 derivative). The *Chonma-ho* has been issued to North Korea's premier armoured formations that would lead the initial attempts to break through South Korean defences. Other armour was relegated to a secondary role in this corps or to North Korea's four mechanized corps. To underscore North Korea's concept of combined arms and the importance of armour, and therefore the importance of the *Chonma-ho*, North Korea's sole armoured corps was directly grouped with two mechanized corps and a single artillery corps. This forms the second echelon of North Korea's deployment to the DMZ, with the first echelon composed of four infantry corps, and the rest in strategic reserve. This may also play a part in a defensive strategy, as the North Korean army has been arrayed in depth, and the armour might be strategically placed to provide both offensive power and a second echelon composed of mobile defences to plug a South Korean breakthrough along the DMZ. The *Chonma-ho* main battle tank – which has at least five variants, usually with different armour thicknesses – constitutes the 'triangle' of North Korean military development: armour, artillery and missiles. This was reminiscent of Soviet military theory, including the application of overwhelming artillery support and the use of large amounts of armour to create a breakthrough after the initial artillery disruption. In that sense, North Korean military strategy is very mobile, and the large number of tanks underscores this. The *Chonma-ho* was an attempt to partially address the technology gap between its dated tank forces and South Korean K1 A1 and the US M1 Abrams tanks. The successor to the K1 A1 is the K2 Black Panther, some of which are already in service; this Hyundai (Rotem) product is believed by some to be the most advanced MBT in the world today.

The biggest changes from the in-depth review of American campaigns are the growth of electronic warfare and the build-up of special forces, already the world's largest at around 200,000 members. Urban, mountaineering and night-time training was expanded. No one doubts the physical toughness of individual special operatives but the quality of training and especially equipment has been questioned by foreign experts.

The army also set up specialist praetorian units. For example, the leader's personal guard, in a dark mustard uniform, used to wear a characteristic X-shaped leather harness that supports a pistol on both sides. A large Guards Command also protects the Kims' extended households.

The KPA's definition of electronic warfare is broad: it includes reconnaissance, code-breaking, intelligence collection and disinformation operations. The main thrust is to disrupt the enemies' C4ISR capabilities while protecting their own.

The DPRK has often been provocative, not least in firing missiles over Japan. It also torpedoed the South Korean corvette, *Cheonan*, killing forty-six sailors, as well as shelling South Korean islands. Fewer than half the shells landed on the islands. Since presumably the north had carefully mapped out the detailed co-ordinates of South Korean and US installations, then judgements on North Korean capabilities – often based on numbers alone – need to be re-assessed. US intelligence reports have often referred to poor leadership, corruption, low morale, obsolescent weapons, weak command and control, as well as poor logistics.

Structure

The size of the armed forces has traditionally stood at fourth in the world behind China, the USA and India. Approximately 5 per cent of the population usually serve as active duty personnel. North Korea has enforced universal conscription for males and selective call-up for women, with many post-service requirements. Active duty personnel size is around 1,190,000 (army 1,020,000; navy 60,000; and air force 110,000; paramilitary 189,000). Traditionally army service lasts between five to ten years and the same for the navy while air force service is about three to four years. Conscription usually begins at 17. The selective service for women is seven years; perhaps the female component of the KPA has reached 22 per cent. In 1993 the service for men was increased to eight to ten years; in 2014 the army conscripts were asked to 'volunteer' for an extra year. This may have been the result of so many children dying of starvation in the 1990s creating a shortage of late teenagers for call-up. It also may have been influenced by the extra work the conscripts have been allocated in civilian projects, ranging from annual collection of crops to special construction projects such as building a large ski resort in the Masik Pass. Young men who are related to senior party officials often escape conscription as have some with bad family connections (*Songbun*). Military service has usually been accepted, despite the tough, even brutal, discipline, because a respectable military record has often been a precondition for a good job and party membership. National service can extend to age 30 and during that period conscripts have usually not been allowed to marry. This has been followed by compulsory part-time service to age 40. Thereafter service continued in the KWA/ Peasant Red Guard to age 60. The active reserve stood at 600,000 while the paramilitary numbered nearly 6 million.[1]

The Military Commission of the Workers' Party of Korea, headed by Kim Jong-un (of course), commands the armed forces. The forces have an egalitarian structure – except for the political leadership. Unlike the UK, where 50 per cent of officers at Sandhurst traditionally went to public school (although this is changing), North Korea is more like the Israeli Defence Force. Nearly everyone starts as a private and works their way up to a possible place in an officers' military academy. Once officers were permitted a fair amount of individual initiative but in the late 1960s the failure of the Second Korean War led to the introduction of political commissars. Since about 2016 there has been a fusion of military and political control between senior echelons of the KWP and the KPA. The

National Defence Commission was the most powerful overall body but in 2015 it was replaced by the Commission for State Affairs.

A complex array of cadet militias for secondary and tertiary students evolved. Military training is mandated on Saturdays on and off campus to help prepare all Korean students for conscription at 17/18 or after graduation as well as for reserve duties in emergencies. The Korean People's Internal Security Forces (KPISF) performed as a national gendarmerie and civil defence force. The KPISF shares the same rank structure as the KPA (except for the most senior ranks) but wears a different uniform.

Defence spending

Official North Korean figures had put the defence budget at just under 16 per cent of GDP in 2010 but foreign experts had reckoned it to be as high as 38 per cent during the 1980s. By comparison, Britain spent about 2 per cent of its GDP on defence and also maintained a nuclear deterrent; but London did not fear a US-led invasion. Under the Kim Jong-un administration, perhaps because of the costs of the strategic nuclear programme, the spending on conventional forces appears to have declined.

The UN named the Korean Mining and Development Corporation (KOMID) as the regime's main arms dealer. Pyongyang has assisted, trained and sold arms to a large number of both insurgents and states as well as instruction in North Korea; KPA trainers have been sent all over the world. A most infamous example was the Zimbabwe National Army's 5th Brigade that committed the *Gukurahundi* massacres in Matabeleland – tens of thousands of innocent Ndebeles were killed by North Korean-trained troops ordered into the area in the first years of Robert Mugabe's rule; the world's media largely ignored the atrocities. Large amounts of Korean military equipment were sold to the Tamil Tiger rebels in Sri Lanka during the long and savage insurgency. It was reported that North Korean pilots fought in the Vietnam War; two KPA anti-aircraft regiments were sent to back up the Hanoi government. North Korea has armed and trained the Palestine Liberation Organization as well as Hezbollah in Lebanon.

Equipment

After the pounding in the Korean War and the later collapse of the USSR, the DPRK forces were less capable than the US-armed and far richer South Korea, so its navy, for example, tended to rely on asymmetric tactics such as midget submarines and human torpedoes. The DPRK also had a large stockpile of ageing chemical weapons: probably 2,500 to 5,000 tonnes.

The KPA also had modern (banned) blinding laser weapons such as the ZM-87. The 'Portable Laser Disturber' was intended to blind humans but also damage range-finders and video-cameras. They were originally produced by the Chinese company Norinco (Northern Industries Corporation). The US had also spent large sums on extensive laser weapons' research as did Israel and Germany, but only Russia, China and North Korea have been reported as deploying them. A battery supplies a portable electric energy converter; it is the size of a heavy machine gun with a gunsight, although lighter versions have been made. The weapons were first displayed in 1995 at defence exhibitions in the Philippines and the Gulf; later in that year they were banned by the UN, however. During the Gulf War of 2003 some British forces were issued with protective goggles because the Iraqis were believed to be using Russian lasers. A handful of American troops were reported to have been injured by laser weapons. In April 1997 a US naval officer suffered a retinal injury consistent with a laser burn by a weapon fired from a Russian freighter, *Kapitan Man*, at a Canadian helicopter in which the American was a passenger. This became known as 'the Juan de Fuca laser incident' because the Russian spy ship was in the Strait of Juan de Fuca in US territorial waters near Port Angeles, Washington. In 2003 North Korea was reported to have used a ZM-87 to illuminate two US Apache helicopters.

The DPRK's cyber warfare has been one of the most advanced in the world. It has been estimated that Bureau 121, the DPRK's main cyber warfare unit, has recruited perhaps as many as 10,000 hackers (far fewer than their Chinese neighbours). Many were based outside North Korea because of better internet connections. Bureau 121 famously hacked Sony in order to stop the company distributing the film *The Interview*, about Kim Jong-un. But hackers also engaged in criminal fund-raising – often they were allowed to keep up to 10 to 25 per cent of their gains; the rest went into state coffers. The KPA has fielded vehicle-mounted jammers with ranges of up to 100 kilometres and has also jammed South Korean military satellites.

Pyongyang allegedly possesses over 1,000 ballistic missiles, according to Seoul. Whether the DPRK has managed to refurbish with missile-launch tubes some of the old scrapped submarines it bought in 1993 has been doubted by US experts. The DPRK had a fleet of perhaps as many as seventy submarines but only about forty were considered functional.

The more conventional armoury includes over 4,000 tanks, 2,500 armoured personnel carriers, plus around 10,000 field artillery pieces and perhaps 5,000 Stalin Organs, multiple rocket launchers. It has a wide array of AA guns and 10,000 MANPADS – Man Portable Air Defence Systems. The navy has around 600 vessels, but very few capital ships. The navy did deploy three old frigates, however. The air force boasts 730 combat aircraft of which under 500 were fighters while the rest are bombers (some are H-5 Beagles). The fighters comprise MiG-23s (Floggers) and MiG-29s (Fulcrums); the helicopters included Russian and Ukrainian Mi-24s (Hinds). The DPRK maintains seventy full-time and contingency airfields. The ground forces have field equipment that is of Second World War or Cold War vintages, but some of the kit for the elite units is far more modern, and sometimes locally manufactured. Most ground forces have been issued with indigenous Kalashnikovs. Front-line troops have been provided with the QJY-88, also known as the Type 88 LMG. This is a 5.8 x 42mm Chinese light machine gun designed in the late 1980s by China North Industries Corporation; the older versions, Type 58 and Type 68, were given to second-tier units. In 2018 a new assault rifle with a grenade launcher, similar to the South Korean S&T Daewoo K11 was seen.

Despite its shortcomings, especially in modern equipment, the KPA in 2019 is a formidable conventional opponent, whether in defence or offence.

Notes

Introduction: The Mouse that Roared
1. Michael J. Seth, *North Korea: A History* (Palgrave, London, 2018) p. 1.
2. John Sweeney, *North Korea Undercover: Inside the World's Most Secret State* (Corgi, London 2014) p. 13.

Chapter 2: The Korean War
1. Quoted in James Goulty, *Eyewitness Korea: The experience of British and American Soldiers in the Korean War* (Pen and Sword, Barnsley, 2018) p. 82.
2. Max Hastings, *The Korean War* (Pan, London, 2010) p. xvi.
3. For a recent book on George Blake's treachery see Steve Vogel, *Betrayal in Berlin: George Blake, the Berlin Tunnel and the Greatest Conspiracy of the Cold War* (John Murray, London, 2019).

Chapter 3: Half War/Half Peace
1. USS *Constitution*, also known as 'Old Ironsides', is a wooden-hulled, three-masted heavy frigate of the United States Navy, named by President George Washington after the United States Constitution. She is the world's oldest commissioned naval vessel still afloat.
2. Jack Cheevers, 'The Pueblo Scapegoat', *Naval History Magazine,* October 2014, Volume 28, No. 5.
3. One of the best military analyses of the second war is a staff paper by Major Daniel P. Bolger, *Scenes from an Unfinished war: Low Intensity Conflict in Korea, 1966–1969* (Leavenworth Papers, No. 19, Fort Leavenworth, Kansas, undated).

Chapter 4: The Leadership
1. Chris Ayres, 'Kim's Baby-Faced Killers', *Sunday Times* magazine, 30 July 2017.
2. Anna Fifield, *The Great Successor: The Secret Rise and Rule of Kim Jong Un* (John Murray, London, 2019) p. 24.

Chapter 5: Nukes
1. For details see Paul Moorcraft, *Total Destruction of the Tamil Tigers: The Rare Victory of Sri Lanka's Long War* (Pen and Sword, Barnsley, 2012).

Chapter 6: Inside the Beast
1. Interview with author, March 2019.
2. Barbara Demick, *Nothing to Envy: Real Lives in North Korea* (Granta, London, 2010).

3. Philip Sherwell, 'Hi-de-hard labour: a sneak peek at Kim's holiday camp', *Sunday Times*, 9 June 2019.

Chapter 7: Daily Life
1. Quoted in Anna Fifield, op. cit., p. 113.
2. Cited in National Geographic: *Inside North Korea*, aired on the History Channel in 2006.
3. Kang Chol-hwan, *The Aquariums of Pyongyang* (Atlantic, London, 2006).
4. Fifield, op. cit., p. 160.
5. One of the best accounts of interviews with defectors is by Barbara Demick, *Nothing to Envy: Real Lives in North Korea* (Granta, London, 2010).
6. John Everard, *Only Beautiful, Please: A British Diplomat in North Korea* (Asia Pacific research Center, Stanford, C.A., 2012) p. 13. Everard was a British diplomat who learned some of the Korean language (and Chinese) and travelled around the country in 2006–08.

Chapter 8: On the Front Line: South Korea
1. Kim Hyun-hee, op. cit.

Chapter 9: Japan – The Old Imperial Power
1. Kang Chol-hwan, op. cit., pp. 30–1.

Chapter 10: The Big Brother – China
1. For a useful summary of the copious Wikileaks data on North Korea see Simon Tisdall, 'Wikileaks cables reveal China 'ready to abandon North Korea', the *Guardian*, 29 November 2010. The *Guardian* was one of the four main Western media outlets that sorted and then publicized the 2010 leaks.
2. Specifically the F-35B STOVL version. *Kaga* and her sister *Izumo* are classed as 'multi-purpose operation destroyers by the JMSDF. An earlier carrier called *Kaga* led the attack on Pearl Harbor.

The Future of Suspicious Minds
1. Michael Palin, *North Korea Journal* (Hutchinson, London, 2019) cover quote.
2. Barbara Demick, op. cit., pp. 67–8.
3. Philip Sherwell, op. cit.
4. See Paul Moorcraft, *Omar al-Bashir and Africa's Longest War* (Pen and Sword, Barnsley, 2016).
5. Andrei Lankov, *The Real North Korea: Life and Politics in the Failed Stalinist Utopia* (Oxford University Press, Oxford, 2016) p. xiv.

Appendix
1. Many of the figures for personnel and equipment have been extracted from the International Institute for Strategic Studies publications, mainly the annuals of the *Military Balance* and *Strategic Survey*.

Select Bibliography

Bolger, Daniel P., *Scenes from an Unfinished war: Low Intensity Conflict in Korea, 1966–1969* (Leavenworth Papers, No. 19, Fort Leavenworth, Kansas, undated)

Demick, Barbara, *Nothing to Envy: Real Lives in North Korea* (Granta, London, 2010)

Everard, John, *Only Beautiful, Please: A British Diplomat in North Korea* (Asia Pacific Research Center, Stanford, CA., 2012)

Fifield, Anna, *The Great Successor: The Secret Rise and Rule of Kim Jong Un* (John Murray, London, 2019)

Goulty, James, *Eyewitness Korea: The experience of British and American Soldiers in the Korean War* (Pen and Sword, Barnsley, 2018)

Hastings, Max, *The Korean War* (Pan, London, 2010)

Jang Jin-sung, *Dear Leader* (Rider, London, 2014)

Kang Chol-hwan, *The Aquariums of Pyongyang* (Atlantic, London, 2006)

Kim Hyun-hee, *The Tears of my Soul* (William Morrow, New York, 1993)

Lankov, Andrei, *The Real North Korea: Life and Politics in the Failed Stalinist Utopia* (Oxford University Press, Oxford, 2016)

Martin, Bradley K., *Under the Loving Care of the Fatherly Leader: North Korea and the Kim Dynasty* (Thomas Dunne, New York, 2006)

Moorcraft, Paul, *Total Destruction of the Tamil Tigers: The Rare Victory of Sri Lanka's Long War* (Pen and Sword, Barnsley, 2012)

——, *Dying for the Truth: The Concise History of Frontline War Reporting* (Pen and Sword, Barnsley, 2016)

——, *Superpowers, Rogue States and Terrorism: Countering the Security Threats to the West,* (Pen and Sword, Barnsley, 2017)

Palin, Michael, *North Korea Journal* (Hutchinson, London, 2019)

Seth, Michael J., *North Korea: A History* (Palgrave, London, 2018)

Sweeney, John, *North Korea Undercover: Inside the World's Most Secret State* (Corgi, London 2014)

Tisdall, Simon, 'Wikileaks cables reveal China ready to abandon North Korea', *The Guardian,* 29 November 2010

Van Tonder, Gerry, *North Korea Invades the South* (Pen and Sword, Barnsley, 2018)

Films

North Korea has spawned numerous fictional films. The best known in the West is the TV series (1972–83) and film called *M*A*S*H* (1970) which was made initially during the Vietnam era and, although amusing, is very unrealistic. The humorous theme was continued by the 2004 animated satirical movie *Team America: World Police* as well as, more recently, *The Interview* (2014), that so incensed Pyongyang.

The state also became a fashionable icon of evil as in the 2002 James Bond film, *Die Another Day*. The Korean War was used by Richard Condon in his 1959 novel, *The Manchurian Candidate*, which generated two film versions in 1962 and 2004.

Both Koreas have shown a keen interest in in movie-making. This book has discussed the extensive efforts of the North Koreans, including Kim Jong-il. The best known example is the Godzilla rip-off, *Pulgasari* (1985), though this should be watched for how *not* to make a movie. A big exception is the excellent 2018 South Korean film, *The Spy Gone North*, directed by Yoon Jong-bin. Set in the 1990s it is loosely based on the true story of Park Chae-seo, a former South Korean intelligence officer who infiltrated the DPRK under the cover of a businessman but he was primarily concerned with finding out about the country's nukes. Although it is a bit dense it does show very realistic aspects of the double bluffs and dangers involved in agent penetration; and the portrayal of Kim Jong-il by Gi Ju-bong is both convincing and creepy. It all looks genuine even though it was filmed in Taiwan, not in Beijing and North Korea.

The DPRK has also inspired many excellent documentaries; one of the most controversial was the BBC's film aired in 2013 made by John Sweeney, although his book on his subterfuge is probably better than the film. The North Koreans make it almost impossible to film anything independently as even the ever-affable Sir Michael Palin found with his 2018 film. One of the most unusual documentaries made was *Dennis Rodman's Big Bang in Pyongyang* (2015).

Index